The Teacher Advisor Program

An Innovative Approach to School Guidance

Robert D. Myrick
Linda S. Myrick

and

Charles Blair
Sally Chambers
Bill Highland
Linda Lawson

Cathy Micheau
Sue Todey
Madonna Wise

ERIC Counseling and Personnel Services Clearinghouse
2108 School of Education
The University of Michigan
Ann Arbor, Michigan 48109-1259

Copyright © 1990 by ERIC Counseling and Personnel Services Clearinghouse

All rights reserved.

ERIC Counseling and Personnel Services Clearinghouse
2108 School of Education
The University of Michigan
Ann Arbor, MI 48109-1259

ISBN 1-56109-003-4

This publication was prepared with partial funding from the Office of Educational Research and Improvement, U.S. Department of Education under contract no. RI88062011. The opinions expressed in this report do not necessarily reflect the positions or policies of OERI, the Department of Education, or ERIC/CAPS.

|ERIC| ®

Contents

Introduction	v
About the Authors	vii
Contributors	ix
Chapter 1: Teacher Advisement: A Developmental Guidance Approach	1
Chapter 2: The Teacher Advisor Program (TAP)	13
Chapter 3: PRIME TIME in Sarasota, Florida Middle Schools *Bill Highland*	31
Chapter 4: OUR TIME in Green Bay, Wisconsin *Sue Todey*	43
Chapter 5: TA Groups in LaPorte, Indiana *Charles Blair*	53
Chapter 6: The Middle School Advisory Program in the Collegiate Schools, Richmond, Virginia *Sally Chambers*	63
Chapter 7: TAP in Pasco County, Florida *Madonna Wise* *Cathy Micheau*	73
Chapter 8: Florida's Model and Pilot Schools *Elizabeth Lawson*	85
Chapter 9: Teacher Questions and Staff Development	95
References	105

Appendix A: Developmental Guidance Units—TAP 109

Appendix B: Roles of School Personnel in TAP 113

Appendix C: Sample Advisement Telephone Call 115

Appendix D: TAP Staff Development 117

Introduction

Counselors today, as never before, are looking for the means to intervene within a school to bring about significant changes in the school environment and the behavior of students within that environment. Current literature abounds with new concepts and ideas. These proposed new approaches, like so many before them, are often replete with catchy slogans and offer "get with it" trendy solutions. It is understandable if some counselors view these proposed reforms as merely another chapter in the large volume of "good ideas" that lack either solid conceptualization or a clear-cut implementation strategy, and are quickly passed over for pages of new, purportedly more promising, innovations.

The Myricks with their Teacher Advisor Program (TAP) are a notable and rewarding exception to the usual trend of innovations that promise much, but deliver little. In TAP they offer a program that has a sound conceptual base in developmental psychology with a field-validated implementation strategy. And it works! Counselors and teachers who have discovered TAP enthusiastically proclaim its effectiveness: TAP transforms students into better learners and better citizens. Counselors and teachers involved in TAP develop more enthusiasm about their work because they can see the results in "turned on" and more effective students. Another, often reported, positive outcome of TAP is more rewarding personal relationships with students.

ERIC/CAPS does not award the crème de la crème classification to a book lightly. Only those few books which offer conceptually sound counseling approaches, that have been validated through successful use in a variety of settings, earn CAPS' highest rating. We have no doubts about the Myrick's Teacher Advisor Program. We truly believe that if the ideas and guidelines presented by the authors are utilized (not to fret, they are not difficult to implement), not only will counselors and teachers enjoy improved relationships with their students, they will also have the satisfaction of observing students who are realizing their full potential. Do we need to ask for anything more?

Garry R. Walz
Director, ERIC/CAPS

About the Authors

Robert D. Myrick is a Professor of Counselor Education at the University of Florida in Gainesville. He is a leading proponent of developmental guidance and counseling and provides a model for a comprehensive program in his popular book *Developmental Guidance and Counseling: A Practical Approach.* In his many journal articles, books and workshops he emphasizes practical approaches for teachers and counselors.

Linda S. Myrick is an Adjunct Professor of Counselor Education at the University of Florida in Gainesville as well as a consultant to school districts, local governments and businesses. She is a former school counselor and district director of guidance. For many years she was a psychologist in private practice working with children and adolescents and their parents.

Contributors

Charles Blair is Assistant Superintendent of Schools for the LaPorte School Corporation in LaPorte, Indiana.

Sally Chambers is a Counselor for the Collegiate Schools in Richmond, Virginia.

Bill Highland is Supervisor of Career Education and Guidance for the Sarasota County Schools in Sarasota, Florida.

Elizabeth Lawson is a Consultant to Florida TAP for the Florida Department of Education in Tallahassee.

Cathy Micheau is Supervisor of Student Services/Guidance for Pasco County Schools in Land O' Lakes, Florida.

Sue Todey is Supervisor of Guidance and Career Education for the Green Bay Area Public School District in Green Bay, Wisconsin.

Madonna Wise is Supervisor of Student Services/Social Workers for the Pasco County Schools in Land O' Lakes, Florida.

Chapter 1

Teacher Advisement: A Developmental Guidance Approach

Introduction

Every successful counseling and guidance intervention used in schools is aimed at developing a young person's potential. While it is difficult to assess the latent talents of every student, most people agree children could achieve more than they do. Developing hidden potential depends on our ability to mobilize untapped resources. The teacher advisement program in middle and high schools is an innovative guidance approach which activates both student and teacher resources and potential.

Many students are doing quite well and enjoy school. They make us proud of our educational institutions. Yet, a great number of the nation's youth feel alienated from school and society. They don't fit a classic image of well-adjusted, hard-working, high-achieving students who reside in All-American families. Instead, they often begin school on a rough and uncertain path that is likely to lead them to dependent, unproductive lives. These are high risk students and they are found in every school district.

High risk students fall into various categories: school dropouts, chronic truants, underachievers, economically disadvantaged, non-English speakers, substance abusers, aggressive delinquents, pregnant teenagers, migrants, physically abused and neglected, and learning disabled. While they may be different in age, sex, or race, live in different communities, attend different schools and have different teachers, they all share a few things in common—they all live under difficult social circumstances, have

While it is difficult to assess the latent talents of every student, most people agree children could achieve more than they do.

problems with school, and struggle with the learning process. The school environment is often unresponsive to them.

We need to assist children in their transition to adulthood. Likewise, we need to help our nation, as it too is in transition and at risk.

> *We need to assist children in their transition to adulthood. Likewise, we need to help our nation, as it too is in transition and at risk.*

- One in five children live below the poverty level. America's childhood-poverty rate is two to three times higher than most other industrialized nations, which offer more generous benefits for the poor.
- One in five children live with one parent, and half of these parents are poor. The number of female heads of household has doubled since 1970 and tripled since 1960. One-third of such women live below the poverty level.
- The teenage pregnancy rate in the United States is the highest of 30 developed nations and has increased 12 percent since 1973. Fifty percent of these girls fail to complete school and earn less than half the income of those who wait to start their families.
- The average public high school today loses 25 percent of it potential graduates. The range of dropouts for states is 11 percent to 44 percent.
- There is a high rate of youth unemployment and a greater threat of prolonged periods of unemployment and low earnings among Black and Hispanic groups.
- By the end of the 9th grade, about 30 percent of all students have experimented with illegal drugs. Before graduating from high school, 90 percent have experimented with alcohol, some use cocaine, and many have become dependent on stimulants.

These and other statistics provide a picture of what it is like for many growing up in America. They highlight changing populations and the daily challenges which face teachers and other educators.

Rescuing a Nation at Risk

It is evident that the United States needs to become more competitive in the national and global marketplace. If we are to compete economically, as well as resolve social problems, then we must do a better job of educating our citizens (Gardner, 1983). Many of our nation's leaders are calling for a complete restructuring of the schools.

What does restructuring mean? If schools are to be reformed, what steps must be taken? And, what are the trade-offs? Realistically, what are the available resources and what are the limitations?

Many of the restructuring proposals are familiar to us: more peer helping, tutoring, smaller classes, small study groups, cooperative learning, self-instruction workbooks, computers and lab equipment, and new or revised curricula. Other suggested changes are more profound and include the way teachers perceive and work with students. For example, the needs and interests of students must be given more consideration and there must be more shared responsibility for helping students learn. More teamwork may be the most essential, realistic, and practical reform available to all schools.

In our high-tech information society, we can no longer prepare students for industrial jobs which demand specific knowledge and conformity. While assembly-line teaching methods are still the norm in many schools, assembly-line jobs are decreasing and are now almost a part of the past. Moreover, we can no longer prepare students as if they were going to live in an unchanging community, unaffected by a global economy or a nation's social unrest. We cannot continue to have a semi-literate workforce which has trouble adjusting to change and communicating with others.

Perhaps reform or innovation should focus less on more education and more on a different kind of education. Harvard economist Robert B. Reich noted that the new engine of American productivity is not fueled by an elite corps of managerial wizards. On the contrary, it is an engine dependent on collaboration—collaboration of workers at all levels. It is this emphasis that must also become a part of any restructuring or reform in the schools. Teachers, especially in the secondary schools, have been encouraged for several decades to be specialists in their respective subject areas, sometimes at the expense of being team players. Too many teachers have drifted into relying on a set curriculum, rather than tailoring it to meet the needs and interests of students. There are, of course, schools using traditional approaches and succeeding even in the most

Many of our nation's leaders are calling for a complete restructuring of the schools.

...we can no longer prepare students as if they were going to live in an unchanging community, unaffected by a global economy or a nation's social unrest.

unlikely circumstances. In these cases, the key elements are almost always the character and commitment of personnel and their ability to work with students. Usually, where school programs are flexible, sensitive and successful, teachers see themselves as part of a team responsible for the total education of their students, not merely a teacher of a particular subject.

The report by a task force of the Carnegie Council on Adolescent Development (1989) emphasized that middle grades have been virtually ignored in the school-reform debates and concluded: "Most young adolescents attend massive, impersonal schools, learn from unconnected curricula, know well and trust few adults in school, and lack access to health care and counseling" (p. 13). Far too many young people feel lost and are vulnerable; an already difficult period of their lives is often made even harder by the nature of our schools.

Far too many young people feel lost and are vulnerable; an already difficult period of their lives is often made even harder by the nature of our schools.

Good Guidance is Good Teaching

For many years, good guidance was considered to be good teaching. Prior to the 1960s most books about school guidance were directed to teachers. There were few counseling specialists and most of them were found in the large urban school districts. When there were no specialists, such as school psychologists, counselors, special education teachers, or social workers, it was a child's teacher who was responsible for helping the child grow personally and socially, as well as academically. This was particularly true in self-contained classrooms, such as those commonly found in elementary schools. However, as children moved into secondary schools, they experienced a greater emphasis on departmentalized subject areas. Teachers were specialized and might see more than 150 students in the course of a day in five or six classes. It was difficult for teachers to know students.

The first wave of high school counselors appeared after Sputnik was launched by the Soviet Union in 1957. They spent most of their time on testing and identifying students who might be encouraged to attend college and become a national asset as a mathematician, engineer, or scientist. In short time, they were asked to go beyond college placement and help with the vocational needs of adolescents. They were also expected to counsel students who had special problems, particularly with school adjustment.

Counselor-student ratios are usually very high, sometimes reaching 1:500. Even in the most favorable working conditions, ratios run as high as 1:200, still making counselors responsible for more students than most teachers are assigned. Consequently, many troubled students have fallen between the cracks and been unable to receive help. Frustrated teachers continue to refer these students for assistance, believing that the counselor has more time, is more skilled and more likely to be effective. Ironically, most counselors are minimally prepared, are overloaded with referrals and have little access to students without disrupting their academic schedules. It is clear that counselors, or other specialists, can not accept total responsibility for guidance and counseling. Good teaching is still, and always will be, the heart of good school guidance.

Good teaching is still, and always will be, the heart of good school guidance.

Three Approaches to Guidance

Crisis approach. When there is a crisis at hand, attention is immediately focused on the situation and treatment. This is a crisis approach to guidance. It is the "fix it up" business, which cannot be avoided on occasion but is also questionable in terms of long-term effectiveness and efficiency.

Prevention approach. There were several governors' conferences on education in 1988 and the emphasis was on prevention. Various Task Forces claimed that an early investment in children could curb the long-term costs of most states in terms of crime, poor health, unemployment, and social ills. They proposed comprehensive and timely prenatal care, health care for young children to prevent diseases and disabilities, and accessible and affordable child day care. They recommended various strategies and were intent on passing legislation which would require school districts to provide special services to high-risk student populations. This prevention approach made more sense than waiting to react with more costly solutions.

Among the recommendations made by the National Governors' Association Task Force on Children (1989) were:

- Developing a tracking system for high risk students.
- Reorganizing large middle schools into smaller, more manageable units, so that young people can gain independence while remaining in a more intimate environment.

- Encouraging schools to create youth-service programs within their curricula.
- Providing more support for families and their children.

In the 1980s more than 1,000 pieces of state legislation were developed which related to education and teacher policies. But, only a fraction of them were approved and implemented. Very often they did not reflect a consensus of opinion and they lacked specific guidelines and funding. Mandating competency-based tests, attendance and course requirements, more graduation credits, or merit money for outstanding teachers, have not proven to be valid solutions.

Developmental approach. Despite the eagerness to solve problems and to improve education, we sometimes lose sight of the most viable concept for helping young people: the developmental approach. This approach recognizes that each individual is unique but progresses through some common growth stages with related needs. It identifies time periods in life when people typically experience extensive changes in their physiological and biochemical systems, which in turn affects their thinking and behavior. Attitudes, habits, and skill development are related to certain stages of development and, if attended to in a positive way, can provide the foundation for future success.

Educational programs, policies, and practices should be developmentally appropriate. We need to know not only what is appropriate but what is effective. What works and what doesn't? What is practical and what isn't? What is cost effective and what is a waste of time? What is workable and what is unrealistic? What can be achieved and what is questionable?

As a starting point, consider the following as criteria to test whether or not schools and educational programs are developmentally appropriate:

- Attention to individual differences in student growth patterns and rates of growth.
- Focus on all aspects of development: physical, social, emotional, cognitive and personal.
- Integrated curriculum rather than isolated skill development.
- Active rather than passive learning.
- Concrete, "hands on" learning materials.

...each individual is unique but progresses through some common growth stages with related needs.

Educational programs, policies, and practices should be developmentally appropriate.

- Small group instruction.
- Multicultural and nonsexist curriculum.
- Peer interaction and group problem solving.
- Heterogeneous grouping of students.
- Flexible strategies for involving students in the learning process.
- Opportunities for decision-making and problem-solving.

Although crisis and prevention strategies will always receive special attention by reformers in education, the approach which incorporates both of them and which makes the most sense is the developmental approach.

The developmental approach in guidance and counseling has been described elsewhere (e.g., Myrick, 1987). Most schools try to develop programs around eight goals. They may be worded a little differently in some school systems or receive a different emphasis, but in general the goals are:

Goal 1: Understanding the School Environment
Goal 2: Understanding Self and Others
Goal 3: Understanding Attitudes and Behaviors
Goal 4: Decision-making and Problem-solving
Goal 5: Interpersonal and Communication Skills
Goal 6: School Success Skills
Goal 7: Career Awareness and Educational Planning
Goal 8: Community Pride and Involvement

Each goal is further delineated by a set of objectives and expected outcomes. These developmental guidance goals are true for all grade levels (K–12).

The Emergence of the Teacher Advisor Program (TAP)

One of the most innovative ways to make sure that all students benefit from developmental guidance and counseling is to directly involve teachers in teacher advisor programs (TAP). Teachers are designated as advisors to groups of 18 to 25 students and meet with their advisees both individually and in group sessions. The group number may be smaller or larger. However, the basic assumption remains the same—each student needs a friendly adult in the school who knows and cares about the student in a personal way.

...each student needs a friendly adult in the school who knows and cares about the student in a personal way.

Elementary school children are, for the most part, in self-contained classrooms and their teachers have more opportunities to know them personally. As students move into middle and junior high schools, they often move from class to class, experiencing more separate classes, more teachers, and a greater number of classmates. This transition is not an easy one and has been a concern of middle school advocates for two decades (Bergman & Baxter, 1983; George, 1986; Kornik, 1984; Patterson & Sikler, 1974).

Middle/Junior High School TAP. The teacher advisor program was first described as a "homebase" or "homeroom" for students when introduced into the middle schools (Alexander & George, 1981; Daresh & Pautch, 1983; James, 1986) during the 1960s. It was assumed that young adolescents faced certain stresses related to their physical and social development which, in turn, affected their educational progress. It was called the age of transescence. There were more choices and decisions to be made. There were more personal and social responsibilities. And, there were more academic expectations, leading to a greater variance in student achievement and progress.

The term "affective education" was popular when middle school teacher advisement programs started in the 1960s and was used to build a rationale for advisor-advisee programs (James, 1986). But, the general public was suspicious about activities which focused on non-academic aspects of education such as self-concept, values clarification, self-disclosure, and moral and social development. Lacking an adequate understanding of developmental guidance and how it was related to helping students learn more effectively and efficiently, most educators were skeptical and failed to systemically develop teacher-based guidance. Advisor-advisee programs, as they were also called then, met with limited success. They were poorly defined in general terms in most textbooks. It was hard to visualize how they would work. Teacher preparation was minimal and there was a general apprehension among teachers, counselors, and administrators. Only the most forward thinking and determined school faculties were able to implement the concept with success.

Alexander and McEwin (1989) completed a 20-year follow-up of an early study by Alexander in 1968 which focused on the restructuring of junior high schools into

The teacher advisor program was first described as a "homebase" or "homeroom" for students....

middle schools. In general, the authors were interested in how schools had progressed in moving from the traditional plan of grades 6-3-3 to 5-3-4. Although there is considerable variance in grade organizations, the general trend was to change junior high schools into middle schools. Approximately 54 percent of 161 schools reported that all teachers in the school served as advisors.

The 1989 study also showed that 77 percent of 181 middle schools scheduled advisory periods five times a week and only 10 percent once a week. The length in minutes and frequency of meetings given over to advisory periods also varied and are shown in Table 1. It was concluded that:

...the general trend was to change junior high schools into middle schools.

> Although comparable data regarding the advisory plans were not collected in 1968, our observations and experiences during the 20-year period, as well as several recent publications regarding advisory plans in the middle school years, are quite conclusive as to the marked growth in number and quality of these plans. This is a positive contribution of middle schools to provision of adult guidance and support at a critical time in adolescent development, a contribution that needs continued expansion, evaluation, and improvement. (Alexander & McEwin, 1989, p. 24)

Several outstanding middle school teacher-advisor programs have been described elsewhere: Northwest Middle School in Greenville, South Carolina (Bohlinger, 1976); Patapsco Middle School in Howard County, Maryland (James, 1986); Webster Transitional School in Cedarburg, Wisconsin (Daresh & Pautsch, 1983; Klausmeier, Lipham & Daresh, 1983); Derby Middle School in Birmingham, Michigan (Mills, 1985); Coolidge Junior High School in Phoenix, Illinois (Klausmeier, Lipham & Daresh, 1983); Noe Middle School in Louisville, Kentucky (Lipsitz, 1984); Shoreham-Wading River Middle School in Shoreham, New York (Lipsitz, 1984; James, 1986); and Sennett Middle School in Madison, Wisconsin (Klausmeier, Lipham & Daresh, 1983).

High School Teacher-Advisor Programs. Developmental guidance and the need for students to have an adult advisor also appealed to some high school faculties. Jenkins (1977) described how Wilde Lake High School in

Table 1
Length and Frequency of Middle School Advisory Periods

Length of Middle School Advisory Periods (1988)

Length in Minutes	Number	Percent
1– 5	6	4
6–10	33	19
11–15	24	14
16–20	36	21
21–25	19	11
26–30	23	14
31–35	3	2
36–40	7	4
41–45	8	5
46–50	5	3
51–55	2	1
56–60	3	2
More than 60	1	1
TOTAL	**170**	**101**

Frequency of Meetings Per Week in Middle School

Number Per Week	Number	Percent
1	18	10
2	17	10
3	5	3
4	1	1
5	140	77
TOTAL	**181**	**101**

Note: From *Earmarks of Schools in the Middle: A Research Report* by W. M. Alexander and C. K. McEwin, 1989, Boone, NC: Appalachian State University.

Columbia, Maryland took the position that guidance was everyone's responsibility. Each teacher worked with 20–25 students in multi-aged groups and was charged with becoming a "significant other" to his or her advisees. School counselors worked closely with the advisee program. Because of teacher assistance in guidance, counselors were freed to work with students who were referred to them with special needs.

Similar advisor-advisee programs were started in other high schools, such as at Ferguson-Florissant High School in Florissant, Missouri. Transition does not stop at the middle school. The educational, personal and social growth needs of students are most effectively met when there is at least one person in the school to whom a student can turn for assistance and when there are opportunities for the student and advisor to come to know each other. The need for teacher advisor programs continues through high school.

In addition to Wilde Lake, other high schools with successful teacher-advisor programs have been described in the professional literature: Cedarburg High School in Cedarburg, Wisconsin (Daresh & Pautsch, 1983); Shoreham-Wading River High School, Shoreham, New York (Goldberg, 1977; Lipsitz, 1984); and Irvine High School, Irvine, California (Klausmeier, Lipham & Daresh, 1983). Organizational structure may vary, but basic assumptions and strategies are the same.

Florida legislators have recognized the value of teacher-advisor programs in both middle/junior high and high schools. Appropriations of about 21 million dollars between 1984 and 1989 have helped fund the development of TAP at the high school level, with specific monies set aside for materials, coordinators, and staff development in more than 100 pilot schools.

The future of our nation depends on educational excellence. We need to have more teachers involved in guidance and advisement. TAP is a valid developmental guidance approach which can help young people realize more of their potential as well as strengthen our nation's human resources.

The need for teacher advisor programs continues through high school.

TAP is a valid developmental guidance approach which can help young people realize more of their potential....

Chapter 2

The Teacher Advisor Program (TAP)

Student and Teacher Needs

Learning, for better or for worse, is a consequence of the learning climate. That climate in a school is created by the interactions of administrators, faculty, support staff, and students. A positive school climate is linked with educational excellence. One way of improving the school environment is through teacher advisor programs (TAP).

Research has documented student problems and teacher concerns. For decades, teachers have consistently worried about students who are disruptive, disrespectful, tardy or absent, and who lie, cheat, deface property and use profane language. Every school has students who are unmotivated, depressed, withdrawn, resentful, discouraged, and who are having conflicts with peers or parents. What can be done with them? Teachers also worry about students who do not follow classroom or school procedures, who are unresponsive to suggestions, and who appear unwilling to change. They are always concerned about school discipline.

Many student problems are part of being at a particular developmental stage in life. Everyone has problems; some are more difficult than others. But to someone who is having trouble, no matter the problem, it is significant and demanding of attention.

There will always be student problems which cannot be solved easily by teachers or other personnel in a school. The problems may be too complex, too intense, or too far-reaching for most school personnel. Yet, these problems are almost always related to dysfunctioning relationships. Even though a school may not have the resources to provide full

A positive school climate is linked with educational excellence.

treatment, it is a starting place. Because a school is the major "home away from home," it can play a significant role in the growing and healing process of a young person.

Student-teacher relationships are central to helping students learn and cope with problems that are part of their developmental stages. But, teachers need help. They need help in understanding students. They need more classroom management skills and new ways of building positive working relationships. They also need to re-examine the kinds of guidance services available to students in their schools and to clarify their roles in a guidance program.

Many teachers are discouraged, according to the second annual Metropolitan Life Poll of the American Teacher by Lou Harris (1985). More than 51 percent of all teachers said that they have considered leaving the teaching profession at some point in their careers. More secondary than elementary school teachers expressed disenchantment with education and appeared more likely to leave.

Interestingly, 75 percent of those who considered leaving, but stayed, did so because of the satisfaction that they derive from their relationships with students! These teachers have many of the same complaints as the teachers who left—inadequate compensation, limited resources, professional treatment, and increasing student needs and problems—but they find teaching young people to be personally rewarding.

In a developmental guidance program teachers are encouraged to work personally with students. More time is available for teachers and students to become better acquainted and there are more opportunities to build close working relationships, which benefit both students and teachers (Myrick, 1987).

In a developmental guidance program teachers are encouraged to work personally with students.

The Teacher and Developmental Guidance

For many years there were so few counselors or other support personnel that the only way students received personal guidance was through their classroom teachers. The first books about school guidance in the 1950s were directed almost exclusively to classroom teachers.

Since the 1960s studies have shown that the way teachers interact with students can make a difference in how well students learn (Flanders, 1965; Wittmer & Myrick,

1989; Purkey, 1970). If teachers are perceived by students as caring and interested in them, they are more likely to be inspired and to enjoy going to school; they feel encouraged and try harder.

Research shows that effective teachers have the same perceived characteristics as effective guidance and counseling specialists. Among these characteristics are the willingness and ability to:

- See the student's point of view.
- Personalize the education experience.
- Facilitate a class discussion where students listen and share ideas.
- Develop a helping relationship with students and parents.
- Organize personal learning experiences.
- Be flexible.
- Be open to trying new ideas.
- Model interpersonal and communication skills.
- Foster a positive learning environment.

Good guidance and good teaching are closely related in terms of a helping relationship.

When students have problems they turn to those who they know are available to them and who they think can offer them the most help. Surveys show that elementary students turn first to their parents and then to their teachers. The majority of adolescents turn first to peers and then to relatives and teachers. In general, the first line of helpers are among those people that students see almost everyday, especially if they have positive relationships with them.

It may come as a surprise to some people but school counselors and other support personnel, who are professionally trained in helping people with personal problems, are not typically a student's first choice of a helper. First, counselors often lack the visibility of teachers or peers. Second, too many times a school counselor's image is aligned with authority, discipline and administrative procedures. While this is changing, counselors still do not have daily contact with most students and, consequently, may not be seen in general as a "friendly advisor or helper."

Classroom teachers have a history of helping students who have personal problems. Some teachers continue to be a source of guidance to their students long after they have

If teachers are perceived by students as caring and interested in them, they are more likely to be inspired and to enjoy going to school....

...counselors still do not have daily contact with most students....

left classes or the school. This is especially true when the teacher-student relationship has been a personal and meaningful one to both parties. To build such a relationship, of course, takes time and a special set of experiences or circumstances.

Popular and assertive students are usually able to establish enduring and helpful relationships with their teachers. Yet, there are many other students who need adult guidance and a mature relationship which they can draw upon. Some students are too shy or withdrawn to reach out to teachers for help. Some students believe they are not liked well enough or cannot compete with popular students for teacher attention. And, some students are aware that their attitudes and behaviors in school are not what is expected and that teachers are not likely to be interested in them.

Teachers are busy people and they often feel burdened with their teaching responsibilities. Their time with students is limited and classroom teachers cannot build close personal relationships with all their students, especially at the secondary level. The reality of school schedules and class arrangements forces teachers to be selective and to pay attention to some students more than others. Favored students receive teacher support and personal guidance while the others must turn elsewhere.

Elementary school teachers have traditionally accepted their roles as guidance teachers. They work in self-contained classrooms and have many opportunities to be aware of student needs and interests. Because they work with the same students for most of a school day, elementary school teachers also have more time to build close relationships and to provide timely developmental guidance.

It is a different story in the secondary schools where teachers work with larger numbers of students and spend limited amounts of time with them. For example, it is not uncommon for many of the core curriculum teachers in junior and high schools to have six classes, with as many as 30 or more students in each class. Thus, a teacher may meet with more than 180 students a day, seeing them for less than an hour in classes where academic skills are emphasized. Thus, it is not surprising that so few secondary school students enjoy the luxury of close working relationships with their teachers.

Some students believe they are not liked well enough or cannot compete with popular students for teacher attention.

Teachers as Advisors

A need exists for teachers to be directly involved in developmental guidance. Perhaps the single most innovative approach to meeting this need is through teacher advisor programs (TAP). TAP is designed to provide all the students in a school an opportunity to be with a small cohesive group (perhaps 15 to 25 peers) led by a sensitive and caring adult. This adult or advisor is usually a teacher in the school who promotes and monitors individual students' educational and developmental experiences as they progress through that school. This has been referred to in various ways: an advisor-advisee program; a home base or homeroom program; an advisement program; advisory meetings; or teacher advisor program (TAP). Some schools have their own logos and special names for the program. Regardless, it is designed to provide continuous adult guidance within a school (Jenkins, 1977).

The need for more advisement by teachers and counselors was supported by a Missouri needs survey. It showed that about 48 percent of the students had not spoken with a school counselor regarding future educational and vocational plans and that only 52 percent believed that the schools had provided opportunities for parents to discuss their child's educational plans. Moreover, 41 percent of the students felt that they did not know one teacher well enough to talk to if they had problems (Johnson & Salmon, 1979).

The teacher as advisor concept was first introduced into the middle schools. Middle schools, following the lead of elementary schools, have placed a greater emphasis on developmental guidance than junior and senior high schools. Students are no longer in one self-contained classroom with one teacher. Instead, they generally work with a team of teachers and are assigned to a homeroom or homebase group where they meet regularly with a teacher-advisor (Alexander & George, 1981).

Who should be advisors? All students, and all faculty and staff members should be involved. Assignments may differ from time to time but all teachers and most available staff should be assigned advisory groups. This makes it possible for a reasonable advisor-advisee ratio and for all

TAP is designed to provide all the students in a school an opportunity to be with a small cohesive group... led by a sensitive and caring adult.

...all teachers and most available staff should be assigned advisory groups.

staff to share equal responsibility for advisement in the school. Local conditions, constraints, and policies will influence who may be advisors.

In some schools, only the building principal and one counselor are not assigned groups. They are expected to be available during TAP time but assume routine duties so that advisory groups can meet with few interruptions. Perhaps the most common approach is to involve only professional faculty or staff, but a few schools have drawn upon other full-time resource personnel as well as volunteers.

Matching students to advisors. Many schools let students select their advisors by indicating choices at the time of registration. Other schools follow random procedures, with special attention given to balancing groups in terms of gender, race, academic ability, and general performance in school. It is wise to make sure any advisor is not overloaded with troublesome students.

Some schools insist that, once assigned, an advisor and an advisory group work together as long as the students remain at the school. It is assumed such continuity enables the group and the advisor to build greater trust and to know each other better. Other schools reassign students to advisors and advisory groups at the beginning of each school year, hoping that students will get to know more than just one group of peers and one adult who has taken the time to know them.

It might make sense to group students with special interests, but keeping all exceptional education students together is not necessarily a good idea. These students need to be mainstreamed in developmental guidance. Likewise, keeping all band students together or those interested in a particular career goal may also be defeating in the long run. Students need a heterogeneous group of peers in their advisory groups.

Some schools have reduced the number of students assigned to each advisor by assigning groups to all but one of their counselors. These groups often consist of those who want to be "peer facilitators" or "peer counselors." Thus, students learn how to help others in the first few weeks of school and then work as peer facilitators.

Responsibilities. Teachers are each assigned, in addition to their academic classes, a group of about 20 students. There may be more or less, depending upon the number of

It is wise to make sure any advisor is not overloaded with troublesome students.

students who attend a school and the number of faculty and staff who are available as advisors. The best ratio appears to be about 1:15; but in practice it as low as 1:8 in a few cases and as high as 1:30 when space and personnel were limited.

It is assumed that each student needs a friendly adult in the school who knows and cares about him or her in a personal way. The advisors help their advisees deal with the problems of growing up and getting the most out of school. The advisor-advisee relationship is the core of guidance in the middle school. TAP has been so well-received by students and parents in the middle schools that it is now being seen as an essential element for guidance in high schools.

A teacher-advisor is usually responsible for an advisee's cumulative folder, work folders, teacher-student conferences, parent conferences, group guidance experiences, and follow-up on academic progress reports. Advisors also consult with other teachers, school counselors and support personnel about their advisees.

Advisory group meetings. Teacher-advisors meet with their advisees on a regular basis through a homeroom or homebase group. The "Homebase" or "Homeroom" period is literally the home within the school for students. It is here that they have a supportive group of peers with whom they can explore their personal interests, goals, and concerns. It is here that issues which get in the way of effective academic learning can be addressed. A guidance curriculum is usually part of TAP and presented during advisory group meetings. Advisory group or homebase periods are about 25-30 minutes in length and often take place at the beginning of each school day. At least two days of the week are scheduled for developmental guidance activities. The other three days are more flexible and might be used for supervised study, tutoring, journal writing, silent reading, mini-courses, clubs, exploration of music and the arts, or for more guidance activities.

Some schools have scheduled homebase meetings in other ways. Scheduling meetings every school day is ideal, since it gives advisors and advisees more opportunities to know each other. It also gives a faculty and staff more opportunities to be creative with those days which are not allotted for group guidance activities.

Regardless, it appears that the homebase period should be no less than 25 minutes if a guidance curriculum is to be

...each student needs a friendly adult in the school who knows and cares about him or her in a personal way.

The "Homebase" or "Homeroom" period is literally the home within the school for students.

Scheduling meetings every school day is ideal....

Advisors tend to rush, lose patience, and give up on group activities when time is short.

delivered with any degree of effectiveness. It simply takes that amount of time to guide students through most structured activities. Time must be managed very carefully and there is a need to be task-oriented. Some guidance activities can not be used if there is not enough time to experience them or discuss their meaning. Advisors tend to rush, lose patience, and give up on group activities when time is short.

Guidance curriculum. When TAP is in place, the guidance curriculum is presented in advisory group meetings. The curriculum may vary, but it is generally assumed that certain guidance experiences can help all students personally, socially, and academically. The curriculum may be organized into guidance units, each with guidance sessions. There are guidance objectives and activities.

Some personal and social skills which often receive attention in the guidance curriculum are: getting acquainted, self-esteem, coping with change, time management, conflict management, and classroom behavior. Academically, topics might focus on policies and procedures from the school handbook, computing grade point averages, finding meaning in test results, developing study skills and habits, standardized tests and test anxiety, and learning styles. A few career and educational planning topics include career exploration and choices, employability skills, the job market, what employers look for, alternative jobs in career fields, job applications, resume writing, and community services.

A developmental guidance unit focuses on a particular topic. Twelve units by topic and general objectives are listed in Appendix A. Other units may be developed in light of special student needs or interests. Some of the units are repeated each year, perhaps with a different set of activities, focus and emphasis. Repetition is helpful in many instances, especially when advisors monitor progress through evaluative instruments.

In addition, the units are organized sequentially in a school's guidance calendar noting the major events of a school year. For instance, an orientation unit might be presented during the first three weeks of school, helping advisees to become more familiar with school facilities, procedures, policies, and resources. This might be followed by a study skills unit, focusing on study habits, test anxiety, and time management. A third unit might be aimed at self-assessment, where advisees think about their classroom behaviors and what must be done if they are to succeed. Personal strengths and areas to improve upon also receive attention.

Each guidance unit might be organized around the general scheme of six sessions (5 + 1). That is, students take part in guidance activities for five sessions and the final session is for evaluation of the unit. A unit can be completed in three weeks, if meetings are held twice a week. If the evaluation in the sixth session shows that objectives were not met or that more time was needed for some skills, then additional sessions can be scheduled.

Advisor skills and preparation. Teachers need special preparation in how to work with their students in guidance sessions and how to build guidance units for their groups. Some sessions are more structured than others. Some are designed to build group cohesiveness and a sense of belonging among the advisees in their homebase period. Other sessions attempt to anticipate the developmental needs of students, while still other sessions depend upon what students want to talk about and the particular needs and interests that emerge.

One teacher-advisor argued that students didn't like or benefit from a study skills unit which had been delivered during homeroom guidance. However, further examination showed that he was depending exclusively upon printed materials and was telling students how to study. The materials were distributed for study during homebase and students answered questions related to them. This teacher missed the point of guidance, was working too hard, and denied students an opportunity to learn from each other.

This teacher was encouraged by a TAP coordinator to put aside the printed materials for the time being and to encourage the group to talk about study habits from their own experiences. It was a time to find out how they approached their homework. What seemed to work for them and what didn't? In addition, advisees might arrive at their own plans based upon information that came out of the group's discussion. This approach makes the topic personally meaningful and more interesting. The handouts might be distributed later when students are ready to examine them. The teacher-advisor needed to learn or relearn and use facilitative teaching skills.

Teachers need special preparation in how to work with their students in guidance sessions and how to build guidance units for their groups.

Counselors and teacher advisors. Teachers, when working as advisors to students, draw upon the skills and resources of guidance specialists such as school counselors (Henderson & La Forge, 1989; Shockley, Schumacker, & Smith, 1984). But, teachers are not considered to be counselors nor is most of their work counseling. Sometimes school counselors may help lead a guidance unit or a session with a teacher-advisor. On other occasions, a counselor may develop a guidance unit and lead a homebase group through some sessions or the unit. Teacher-advisors, recognizing their own limits in terms of their time available and their skills, can identify students who need attention from a counselor or other specialist.

Working together, counselors and teachers can define their respective roles in guidance and differentiate responsibilities. A brief outline of roles is found in Appendix B. Where developmental guidance programs are successful, teachers and counselors work as a guidance team.

TAP: An Essential Guidance Program

The same concepts that have proven their value in the middle schools also make sense for high schools. In fact, we can use the term TAP (Teachers as Advisors Program) to refer to either a middle or high school guidance program which involves teachers working with groups of students as advisors.

Although developmental stages and tasks are different for older adolescents, there is still a need for developmental guidance and to assist students in their intellectual, social, and personal growth. There may even be a more pronounced need to personalize and humanize education.

The Ferguson-Florissant School District in Florissant, Missouri, started a high school advisement program that was part of a project funded by the Kettering Foundation. The program was later revised and expanded under Title IV-C funds and subsequently became a model program for many other school districts. The organization and the materials helped teachers provide more guidance services to students. Other high school programs were started about the same time in such states as Maryland, New Jersey, Florida, and Georgia and helped demonstrate the value of TAP in high schools.

...teachers are not considered to be counselors nor is most of their work counseling.

...counselors and teachers can define their respective roles in guidance and differentiate responsibilities.

Many high school teachers have never had a guidance course and many are unsure of how to lead a group discussion with adolescents when there is no lesson to be taught. It is difficult for them to put aside old teacher modes and habits and to become better listeners and facilitators. Many are uncertain as to how to use TAP time and far too many do not understand the basic principles of developmental guidance and TAP. Consequently, it is not uncommon for a beginning teacher advisor program to initially meet with teacher skepticism, apprehension and resistance.

The Counselor's Role in TAP

Counselor and teacher-advisor roles are complementary but different. First, teachers are not asked to be counselors or to assume full responsibility for meeting all the counseling and guidance needs of students (Pilkington & Jarmin, 1977; Trump, 1977). Some students will be referred to counselors or other specialists because advisors are limited in skill and time. Second, counselors will continue their own counseling programs and activities throughout the school day, but during TAP period they will probably pay particular attention to the following roles:

1. Counselors can co-lead some guidance units and sessions with teachers. Some teachers will invite counselors to work with them on occasion, including teachers who are very successful. At other times, counselors will work with teachers who are having trouble managing their groups. Counselors might model group guidance skills or serve as a consultant to these teachers.
2. Counselors can develop special guidance units based on particular needs of a student group or student population. For example, in one middle school older students were bullying younger students and counselors prepared a four-session guidance unit which they presented to homebase groups. In another school, some racial slurs increased the potential for student violence and the issue was addressed through a special guidance unit. In a sense, these counselors developed a "road show" which they took to the TAP groups.

...it is not uncommon for a beginning teacher advisor program to initially meet with teacher skepticism, apprehension and resistance.

...counselors developed a "road show" which they took to the TAP groups.

3. Counselors can meet with small groups of students for small group counseling. If TAP is a regularly scheduled period in the day, counselors can meet with students at that time and are less disruptive of academic classes in order to have small group counseling sessions with students. Counselors in the middle and high schools, for example, sometimes report how difficult it is to have students released from their classes, and there are few opportunities to meet students in groups without a lot of scheduling problems.
4. Counselors can pull students who are targeted for special attention from their homebase group during TAP time. Some students may have trouble adjusting to their advisory group or be disruptive. These students might receive small or large group guidance and counseling experiences which focus on their problems. In another situation, students might need to obtain and discuss information or guidance materials that affect them more than other students. For example, specific college information or job opportunities might be topics for groups who meet with counselors during TAP time, especially on those days when the teacher-advisor is not presenting a guidance unit.
5. Counselors can meet with some students for individual counseling. In general, individual counseling is usually reserved for other times during the day since it is easier to draw individuals from academic classes than groups. Therefore, the counselor's work emphasis during TAP is on small and large groups, either with a teacher-advisor group or with a special group organized by the counselor.
6. Counselors can serve as consultants and personal resources to teachers about TAP. If a full- or part-time TAP coordinator is not employed in a school, it is common for a school counselor to assume leadership and coordinate TAP. This might be done with a teacher as a co-leader or through a steering committee.
7. Counselors can use TAP time to organize a peer facilitator training program. A counselor might train a group of peer helpers to work in such roles as

teacher-assistant, tutor, special friend, or small group leader. Teacher-advisors can then draw upon these students to help them lead group discussions in their advisory groups or to help their advisees individually.
8. Counselors should avoid any routine duties during TAP time which takes them away from working with teachers or students. Teachers want counselors to be part of TAP and to be available and visible during that time.

Building Support for TAP

Despite the apparent value of TAP, there are middle/junior and high school teachers who are reluctant to support it. In general, about 20 percent of most secondary school faculties will quickly embrace the program. These teachers like the idea of developmental guidance and they have the skills and personality to put the program in practice without much preparation. They can make it work with a minimum of support, as they thoroughly enjoy the opportunity to form closer helping relationships with students.

There is another 20 percent of a school faculty, in general, who are clearly resistant. They argue against it and see only an extra preparation for themselves. To them TAP is a waste of time. They erroneously believe that guidance should be left to specialists, such as counselors and school psychologists. This reluctant group of teachers needs special assistance or inservice training, if they are ever to be supportive and become involved in building a program. Unfortunately, of this 20 percent of resistant teachers probably half of them do not have the personality, skills, interests, or energy to make TAP work and they may need to be assigned other duties.

The middle 60 percent of the faculty makes the critical difference. If this group is for TAP, then the program will make a positive contribution in the school. If the majority of teachers are against TAP, then the program will have trouble surviving; it will be sabotaged. There will be a tremendous waste of time and energy. Student needs will not be met and, being disappointed with TAP, students will "add fuel to the fire" by their criticisms and lack of interest.

Counselors should avoid any routine duties during TAP time which takes them away from working with teachers or students.

Critical Factors for Success

What factors are most critical to enlisting the support of 60 percent of a school's faculty for TAP and developmental guidance?

Understanding the philosophy of TAP. This includes an understanding of student needs and an awareness of student problems. It also includes a recognition of how guidance is directly related to helping students learn more effectively and efficiently in their academic work, as well as helping them grow socially and personally.

Can teachers explain the program to others? What words do they choose to emphasize? What would they say about TAP in three minutes? Are their statements student-centered or self-centered?

Committing adequate time for TAP. Some teacher advisor programs suffer because there is not enough time for advisors to meet with their advisees. There is little chance that caring and helping relationships will develop if meeting times are limited, sporadic, or lacking in continuity. When advisors meet with advisees on an irregular basis, there is little chance to implement guidance activities with any consistency. This influences teachers' and students' attitudes and reflects the value given to the program.

TAP works best when it is scheduled every school day. This gives advisors an opportunity to know their advisees and to talk with them individually as well as in groups. During supervised study time, teachers can work with student folders and make plans to follow up with other teachers.

TAP must be scheduled a minimum of two days a week; otherwise there is a tendency for a faculty to view TAP as an unimportant adjunct program rather than an integral one with a curriculum. It is difficult to feel committed to a program that is not part of the regular weekly schedule. When it pops up on occasion in the school schedule, teachers tend to think about it less and rely on whatever spontaneously happens. As one teacher said, "I just wing it and hope for the best." Without a weekly commitment, teachers are less concerned about how they can best use the TAP period with students, since that time is such a small part of their assignment. This kind of situation inevitably sows seeds of discontent among teachers and students and results in unneeded conflicts.

There is little chance that caring and helping relationships will develop if meeting times are limited, sporadic, or lack continuity.

TAP must be scheduled a minimum of two days a week....

Providing a developmental guidance curriculum guide. Teachers are used to having curriculum guides and they often depend on learning activities to stimulate student thinking and participation. Teachers like to have organized guidance handbooks which contain various activities that they might use in TAP.

Some schools have developed a comprehensive set of materials, including guidance units, and recommend when they might best be used during TAP. Teacher-advisors have the liberty of discarding any suggested activity that seems unsuited for them or their group, perhaps modifying an activity or substituting another one. The evaluation of the unit can remain consistent across all TAP groups. Thus, the guidance objectives are more important than any activity and it is an advisor's professional judgment which determines how best to meet those objectives.

Preparing teachers in guidance and interpersonal skills. Since most teachers have not had a course in guidance, many do not know how a guidance program is developed to meet student needs and how guidance interventions can be used to help students. Teachers may have limited conferencing skills and many are unsure of how to manage groups in an open discussion. More specifically, far too many teachers rely on one group arrangement—all students facing the front of the room—and need more training in how to get students working cooperatively in small groups.

Many teachers also need to know how to help students think about a personal problem and to take some steps in solving a problem. This does not mean that the advisor is the problem-solver; rather, the advisor helps students explore situations, alternatives and consequences, and possible plans of action.

The basic skills which teacher-advisors need to study, review, and practice are: responding to students' feelings, clarifying or summarizing ideas, asking open-ended questions, complimenting and confronting, linking feelings and ideas, setting limits, and acknowledging contributions (Wittmer & Myrick, 1989). There are many interpersonal communication models which can be useful and it may be valuable to have all advisors in a school become familiar with at least one which they all know and have experienced.

Having visible administrative support. Most administrators try to accommodate their teachers and to make teaching enjoyable. Teaching is not easy work. Some

...teachers...need more training in how to get students working cooperatively in small groups.

students, and teachers as well, can dampen the spirit of a school. These students and teachers make everyone's work more difficult and the school environment unappealing.

Because administrators so often set the tone of a school through their personal styles and commitment, they are the glue which holds programs together. If they are supportive, then teachers will try harder. If they are indifferent, then teachers find other places to invest their time and energy. Therefore, they must not only speak favorably about TAP, but they must take time to understand how TAP works and to find ways to demonstrate their support.

Administrators can increase their visibility in the schools by visiting TAP groups and talking with students when discipline is not an issue. They talk with TAP coordinators about guidance units and, on occasion, they might co-lead or lead a discussion in one of the TAP homerooms.

Evaluating and assessing TAP. In order for TAP to be an accountable program it must be monitored and evaluated. Evaluations provide data upon which to make decisions and to select new directions, if any, to be taken. Student and teacher evaluations of TAP are essential.

It takes time to develop an excellent program: Adjustments must be made, new things added and other things deleted. Priorities must be set and people must learn to work together. With feedback from students and teachers, it is possible to keep TAP moving in the desired direction.

Teachers: The Heart of Developmental Guidance

There are not enough school counselors, or other specialists, to implement a developmental program, if they have the sole responsibility for guidance. Only with teacher involvement and commitment, at all grade levels, is developmental guidance possible.

Teachers are the heart of a school's guidance program. They work directly with students in their classes and student-teacher relationships influence the school atmosphere. They work as student-advisors and they collaborate with other specialists to assist students.

Counselors support teachers in their work. They work for and with teachers. They need teacher assistance if they are to fully understand a student's world. They also need teacher cooperation if they are to have access to students for

---

...administrators so often set the tone of a school through their personal styles and commitment, they are the glue which holds programs together.

Only with teacher involvement and commitment...is developmental guidance possible.

their own interventions. In order for counselors to excel in their work, school faculties must understand the nature of a counselor's job and how counselor job functions are related to the work of teachers and other specialists.

Teachers and counselors must work together as a team in order to provide a comprehensive developmental guidance program. Developmental guidance and counseling services are essential factors in the pursuit of educational excellence.

...school faculties must understand the nature of a counselor's job....

Chapter 3

PRIME TIME in Sarasota, Florida Middle Schools

Bill Highland

Getting Started

The Sarasota County School System is located on the Florida Gulf Coast, about 50 miles south of Tampa. It serves 26,000 students grades K–12, enrolled in 36 regular and alternative schools. There are five middle schools (grades 6–8) and one alternative middle school. In 1980 the school system undertook a careful study of teacher advisement programs while attempting to determine the merits of middle schools. During the 1982–83 school year, all of the county's five junior highs were reorganized into middle schools (grades 6–8) and the teacher advisor program was seen as an integral part of the philosophy and basic plan.

A daily 30-minute advisory period, called PRIME TIME, was scheduled in each of the middle schools. This created a special time during each school day when students could meet with a caring adult, as well as participate in peer group activities related to personal, social, and academic growth. It was clear from literature reviews and visitations to other middle schools that a teacher advisement program was essential to the kind of middle school programs the district wanted for its students.

Because the restructuring of schools was extensive and made a lot of demands on all school personnel, it was decided to schedule a 30-minute period for silent reading during the first year. Thereafter, it became known as PRIME TIME and more attention was given to the guidance components of the program. This first year was considered a

A daily 30-minute advisory period... created a special time during each school day when students could meet with a caring adult.

luxury to those responsible for developing a plan for advisement and for outlining the direction in which the program would move. They wanted time to plan.

What Were the First Steps in Getting Started?

Step 1. In 1982, a four-member administrative team was formed to coordinate a study of teacher advisor programs. It consisted of county supervisors and directors of curriculum, staff development, and guidance. They began by developing a plan of preparation for the year, including a budget.

The team reviewed related literature on advisement in the middle school and sent letters to schools in the nation with existing programs, requesting information and copies of materials. They attended state and national seminars/workshops on middle schools and talked with nationally recognized experts.

Step 2. The administrative team, with selected teachers and counselors, traveled to other middle schools where they observed advisement programs in action. Two highly successful middle school counselors from Gainesville, Florida were invited to lead a two-day workshop with "new" middle school counselors; time was also used to clarify the counselor's role in advisement.

Step 3. A consultant in middle school education from the University of Florida was invited to speak with each of the five middle school faculties. He outlined the need for advisement and some of the advantages and outcomes.

Step 4. An eight-member committee was responsible for developing the *PRIME TIME Handbook*. In addition to three county staff supervisors, each of the five middle schools had a representative, either a teacher or counselor. The school-based staff were paid a stipend for off-duty time and provisions were made for substitutes on school days when the committee met to work together.

The first edition of the handbook was developed in a "cookbook" format which included hundreds of suggested group guidance activities based around some common themes. Advisors could pick activities from the handbook to use with their group of advisees. The handbook has since evolved into a more structured approach with one book for each grade level (6, 7, and 8). Some activities were modified, others were eliminated, and some new ones have been added.

Step 5. Inservice and staff development activities related to advisement were planned for middle school teachers and counselors. In order to provide some initial preparation to all faculty, a 10-module (30 minutes each) skill development package was presented to 25 (five from each school) selected middle school staff in a workshop in June of 1983. After experiencing the modules themselves, these staff members, working as training teams in their schools, were coached in how to deliver the same modules to their respective faculties at various times over the next few months. The preparation modules proved to be effective (Myrick, Highland, & Highland, 1986).

During August of 1983 a two-day workshop, prior to teachers' regular pre-school days, was scheduled in nine sessions. Two of the ten skill development modules were presented in two sessions. Five sessions of "show and tell" by pairs of successful middle school advisors were included. There was one session on parent conferencing and another session on how to use the handbook. There was also a question and answer period at the end of the workshop. A total of 270 staff members were broken into nine groups of 30 each. These groups then rotated through the nine sessions.

Step 6. A tri-fold brochure describing PRIME TIME was prepared for parents and distributed through the mail to the 5700 homes of middle school parents at the beginning of the 1983–84 school year and they were encouraged to talk with school personnel about their questions or concerns. Only one parent called to complain, thinking the program was "a waste of time." It was learned quickly that most parents liked the idea and were supportive.

Step 7. PRIME TIME was fully implemented in the fall of 1983. Teachers were asked to assess the program and make recommendations for change. A six-member committee of district personnel developed a supplement to the *PRIME TIME Handbook* in the summer of 1984 called *PRIME TIME Makes a Difference!* This was a compilation of best practices and answers to common questions and concerns by teachers. A mini-workshop was held in each school to distribute and review its contents.

Each year a workshop related to teacher-advisor programs is held for all teachers new to the district. Writing teams from the schools have met during the summer to examine the program and identify or develop new guidance activities for the advisory program.

A tri-fold brochure describing PRIME TIME was prepared for parents and distributed through the mail to the 5700 homes of middle school parents....

What Were Some of the Initial Problems?

As the district entered the first year of implementation the enthusiasm for PRIME TIME was high and the initial feedback was positive. Some teachers, of course, were less sure and more skeptical. Some teachers had more trouble than others in making the best use of their time with advisees and some lacked experience in leading guidance activities.

The specific concerns expressed during the first year, based on some evaluation sessions held in the spring of the year, focused on how to use the handbook, where to go for support, how to involve parents, when to transfer an advisee to another advisory group, how to maintain control of less cooperative advisees, how to get kids to talk more, and why grades are not given.

The district administration was so committed to having PRIME TIME that even the most skeptical and resistant of teachers were swept into the mainstream of working hard to make the program work. Yet, genuine concerns had to be addressed beyond large group workshops and general staff development procedures. Skill levels differed among teachers, which contributed to the varied levels of success of the different advisory groups.

The district administration was so committed...even the most skeptical and resistant of teachers were swept into the mainstream....

PRIME TIME

PRIME TIME is under the direction of the Supervisor of Career Education and Guidance Services at the district level. At the school level it is under the direction of the building principals, including an alternative middle school. The principal generally designates a person on the staff to be responsible for coordinating the program.

How is the Program Scheduled?

PRIME TIME meets five times per week, usually the first 30 minutes of the school day. Some schools, because of unusual scheduling problems, have elected to use other time periods during the day.

Developmental guidance is considered to be a central focus of the program and is generally scheduled for two of the five days, but it may be scheduled for three days if desired by an advisor or if it appears to be particularly timely. The remaining 3 (or 2) days are used for silent reading, journal writing, improvement of study skills, intramural sports, work with peer facilitators, or special projects.

How Are Students and Advisors Matched?

Middle school faculties are organized into teaching teams. A typical team consists of four teachers who are responsible for about 120–130 students. Two additional teachers (e.g., Exploration, Physical Education, Exceptional Student Education) are also assigned to a team for PRIME TIME, which creates groups of 20–23 advisees.

The matching of advisors and advisees varies from team to team and school to school. Sometimes students pick teachers as advisors and in some cases, teachers pick students. Sometimes students are assigned alphabetically and in other instances they might be assigned randomly. The matching process is a team decision.

Is There a Guidance Curriculum?

The curriculum for PRIME TIME has evolved over a period of years. The first handbook for advisors was a collection of group activities drawn from about ten different advisement programs in the state and nation. Based on teacher feedback the second and third editions of the handbook have become more structured with sequential activities and related student outcomes or objectives. This handbook is designed around seven guidance themes.

The curriculum is based on assumptions about the social, emotional, and psychological development of students in grades 6–8. Some recognized student needs at this stage of growth are: to be trusted and respected; to be safe and secure; to be accepted and have friends; to be understood; to be able to communicate with others; to be self-confident and independent; and to be successful. PRIME TIME expected student outcomes are:

- To apply knowledge of school rules, facilities, and personnel to everyday functioning.
- To understand academic requirements and the relationships between academics and future success.

...curriculum is based on assumptions about the social, emotional, and psychological development of students in grades 6–8.

- To demonstrate ways of coping/getting along with others.
- To develop feelings of self-worth.
- To demonstrate effective interpersonal skills.
- To demonstrate a knowledge of careers and employability information and skills.
- To demonstrate positive thinking and skills related to goal setting.

To achieve these outcomes there are seven PRIME TIME units focusing on: Orientation; Study Skills and Educational Planning; Getting Along With Others; Positive Thinking and Goal Setting; Self-Worth and Peer Pressure; Career Exploration and Employability Skills; and Interpersonal Skills. The units are usually delivered twice a week for 36 weeks, totalling about 72 guidance sessions per year. The program is planned around a 36-week school year or 180 days. Each advisor is given the flexibility of how and when to best present the units, including the number of sessions. Table 2 shows the recommended sequence of units for each of the three grade levels, including the suggested number of sessions and school weeks.

What Are the Advisors Responsibilities?

The *PRIME TIME Handbook* lists five responsibilities for advisors. In general, they are:

1. Know each advisee in his/her group on a personal basis.
2. Know the parents/guardians of advisees and facilitate communication between home and school.
3. Facilitate cohesiveness in the advisory group.
4. Plan and use activities to implement the guidance goals and objectives of the Advisory Program.
5. Seek out assistance for advisees whose needs are beyond the advisor's ability or time to help.

Teacher advisors are encouraged to be an advocate for their advisees and to gain their trust through activities which develop a feeling of caring.

Modeling good listening and respect for individual uniqueness is important.

Teacher advisors are encouraged to be an advocate for their advisees and to gain their trust through activities which develop a feeling of caring. Advisors should be willing to share their own feelings and personal experiences when appropriate and participate in activities with students. Modeling good listening and respect for individual uniqueness is important. Ownership for the program and outcomes

Table 2
Sequence of PRIME TIME Units

6th Grade Sequence

	Student Outcomes	Sessions	School Weeks
#1	Orientation	8	1–4
#2	Study Skills	11	5–9
#3	Getting Along With Others	8	10–13
#7	Positive Thinking/Goal Setting	10	14–18
#4	Self-Worth - Peer Pressure	20	19–28
#6	Career Exploration	16	29–36
Total		73	

7th Grade Sequence

	Student Outcomes	Sessions	School Weeks
#1	Orientation	4	1–2
#2	Study Skills	8	3–6
#4	Self-Worth	21	7–16
#7	Positive Thinking/Goal Setting	6	17–19
#5	Communication Skills	12	20–25
#3	Getting Along With Others	12	26–31
#6	Career Exploration	12	32–36
Total		75	

Table 2 (Continued)
Sequence of PRIME TIME Units

8th Grade Sequence

Student Outcomes	Sessions	School Weeks
#1 Orientation	4	1–2
#2 Study Skills (first part)	6	3–5
#3 Getting Along With Others	12	6–11
#7 Positive Thinking/Goal Setting	12	12–17
#2 Educ. Planning Unit (second part)	10	18–22
#5 Communication Skills	8	23–26
#4 Self-Worth	8	27–30
#6 Employability Skills	12	31–36
Total	**72**	

Note: The Student Outcome #2 is divided in 8th grade into Study Skills and the Educational Planning Unit (getting ready for high school).

Reprinted from *PRIME TIME Handbook*, Sarasota County Schools, Sarasota, Florida.

must be shared with the group members and opportunities for decision-making must be allowed.

More specifically, advisors are responsible for creating a cohesive working group. Student movement on campus is at a minimum during PRIME TIME. It is not a time to return library books or to run errands. Mondays and Fridays are usually reading days but this is not viewed as a study hall. Advisors also request the services of volunteer helpers, guest speakers, and other resource personnel when appropriate. Videotapes related to guidance outcomes may be used.

Selected peer facilitators are scheduled for one advisory group, where they receive training and supervision in projects which are often related to PRIME TIME activities. After training and through coordinated efforts, peer facilitators work with other students as tutors or special friends and assist in group advisory activities.

Because PRIME TIME is a home base for students, advisors attempt to make a brief parental contact early in the school year (e.g., phone call, letter, advisory breakfast) forming a link between home and school. Student progress reports and report cards are distributed during PRIME TIME. Advisors are included in parent conferences held at the school, which are usually held in a regularly scheduled 30-minute "duty" time at the end of the day. If a conference is held at another time and the advisor is not available, the advisor provides a written report which might be used with the parents.

Special Features

In addition to organized guidance sessions two or three days a week, students learn to know each other better through various activities and projects. These provide opportunities to study and practice communication and interpersonal skills.

Journal writing is an activity which often takes place during PRIME TIME. The experience provides students an opportunity to put their ideas and feelings into words at least once a week. They may write in their personal notebooks about anything they choose without concern for being evaluated. They may describe what they did yesterday, what they are doing today, an event, or some feelings that they have about something or someone. The journals are stored in a safe place by the advisors. After reading a journal, the advisor simply initials or stamps it and may write a helpful response.

Sometimes journal topics are selected by the advisor, and this gives advisees a chance to say in writing what they have trouble saying aloud. It is generally understood that students may choose whether or not they want the advisor to read what they have written. For example, students may fold

...students learn to know each other better through various activities and projects.

the pages of their journals or staple certain pages together to indicate that the information is private.

Silent reading is another popular activity for days during PRIME TIME when guidance activities are not being presented. Students sit quietly in their seats and read whatever they choose. This program encourages reading for enjoyment. Every student is asked to have reading materials on the school's designated days for this activity. All teams have available a supply of high interest paperback books. No one talks aloud or does unrelated tasks.

Some students have poor reading skills or a short attention span. Advisors may try to enhance the experience by providing motivational reading materials such as newspapers, selected magazines, short biographies or stories. Media specialists and reading resource teachers can help provide suitable materials for students who need help and in some cases, materials may be selected because of a particular student concern or problem.

In a PRIME TIME advisory group, students also learn through fun and thoughtful group activities. Round-robin games, for example, create a feeling of unity, openness to sharing ideas, and understanding of self and others. Games such as soccer, kickball, volleyball and softball have been played on some days. Board games based on trivial pursuit or vocabulary skills have helped students learn to work and play together.

Some PRIME TIME groups have organized themselves to help in projects outside the school. One project involved visiting nursing homes and making small gifts or cards for the residents. Another project involved collecting canned food for the needy families in the community and still another focused on ecology and energy conservation. Awareness activities are popular, such as the time when students promoted school and community activities related to the annual "Smoke Out" campaigns.

Within-school projects are also developed by students. One school focused on growing and caring for plants on the campus and taking care of school bulletin boards and assemblies. A team or school-wide talent show has been organized by advisory groups and in some cases PRIME TIME groups within a team have presented a play or role-play situations to other teams and other grade levels. Students with special skills or hobbies are encouraged to share their experiences during advisory times.

In a PRIME TIME advisory group, students also learn through fun and thoughtful group activities.

Several activities are related to helping students feel special about themselves and the value of recognizing others. Friendship awards are filled out by group members and given to others in their advisory group. Birthdays are celebrated. Some groups plan and prepare a meal together, perhaps an international dinner or lunch. Advisors strive to make sure each student is recognized for his or her contributions.

Communication with parents is an important feature of PRIME TIME. A sample of an advisement call is shown in Appendix C. Although brief, it is designed to let parents know that their children are attending a school where teachers care and are interested in parental involvement.

Materials describing PRIME TIME have been shipped to many school systems throughout the nation, as well as foreign countries. Copies of these materials may be obtained through the National Resource Center for Middle Grades Education in Tampa, Florida. Sarasota has also hosted many educators who are interested in seeing how the program works.

One of the schools, Sarasota Middle School, has been designated in the state of Florida as a "model middle school for advisement." It serves designated pilot schools in the state which are in the process of developing and implementing advisement programs.

...an advisement call...is designed to let parents know that their children are attending a school where teachers care....

What Key Factors Have Contributed to the Program's Success?

There may be a number of factors which make for success or failure of a middle school advisement program, but five key factors are:

1. The principal. The principal must not only support the concept but must know the philosophy behind the program. He or she must be able to describe it, discuss it, and give examples of how it works in a brief period of time. Teachers, students, parents, and community members will ask questions of the principal and they expect some answers. The most successful principals are sensitive to the needs and interests of their faculty, have provided opportunities for staff development, work cooperatively with a faculty steering committee, and observe advisement groups on a regular basis.

2. The counselor. School counselors play a key role in advisement by helping in staff development, supplying supplementary guidance activities, and working diligently on steering committees. They identify and help teachers who need assistance. They are available for follow-up and referrals. They take an active leadership role and have high positive visibility.

3. Staff development. Prior to implementation of an advisement program there should be some careful preparation of teachers as advisors. Inservice programs should focus on communication skills and leading group discussions. Skills should be presented, demonstrated, and practiced. New staff need to be introduced and made aware of the concepts associated with advisement. Experienced staff need opportunities for renewing and refreshing their skills and perceptions.

Inservice programs should focus on communication skills and leading group discussions.

4. Materials. Asking teachers to find and/or to develop their own materials and activities for their advisory group meetings is tantamount to guaranteeing failure in most schools. Successful schools have materials readily available and advisors feel supported in their work.

5. Steering committees. A steering committee accomplishes several objectives. It provides a sense of ownership to the faculty and it provides a means for feedback which can be used for confirmation or change. The committee shares ideas, identifies successful components, helps evaluate the program, and suggests new directions.

Successful schools have materials readily available and advisors feel supported in their work.

What Advice Do You Have for Those Who Are Starting?

First, take a close look at the five factors of success and make sure that they receive attention. Begin with the principal, whose role and attitude is perhaps the most important element.

Answer the questions posed by teachers and parents as best you can at the time and be prepared to answer them again in the future, perhaps with more information received through experience. Building an outstanding program takes time and patience. There must be a concentrated effort by administrators, counselors, and teachers, but the rewards are commensurate.

Chapter 4

OUR TIME in Green Bay, Wisconsin

Sue Todey

Introduction

The Green Bay Area Public School District is a unified district of 92 square miles which covers the City of Green Bay, Wisconsin, and all or part of several neighboring towns. It is the fourth largest district in the state, with over 17,000 students enrolled in 23 elementary schools, four middle schools, and four high schools.

The district has a teacher advisor program in all four middle schools called OUR TIME. It is considered an integral part of each school's total program. The development of this approach to advisement resulted from careful study and was part of the movement to change the district's four junior high schools to middle schools.

...a teacher advisor program...called OUR TIME...is considered an integral part of each school's total program.

Getting Started

In 1981, a Middle School Study Committee, consisting of 20 school staff and community members, studied the middle school concept and recommended it for adoption. This recommendation was further supported in 1983 when a 2001 Committee, composed of 24 community members and school staff, also confirmed the idea. By 1984, a Transition Team was appointed by the superintendent to develop specific plans for an advisory program.

The goals of the Transition Committee were to design a program which would address the developmental needs of all students and to promote equal educational opportunities so that each student could discover and develop his or her unique abilities. The plan was to involve all certified staff in order to create the kind of caring environment which was the essence of the middle school concept.

What Were the First Steps in Getting Started?

Step 1: The first three committees (1981–1984) lay the foundation for including an advisory program in the middle schools. In 1985 an Implementation Team (eight teachers and six administrators) was formed to provide district leadership. A Middle School Advisory Program Committee (two counselors, five teachers, and three administrators) was appointed as a subcommittee of the Implementation Team. This committee outlined the philosophy, goals, and general format of the program. It also described the roles and responsibilities of staff in relation to the program. It collected and reviewed resources, refined objectives and a guidance curriculum, and arranged for public relations activities. The committee also made arrangements for in-service training.

Step 2: Implementation of the advisory program in the middle schools was delayed until the third year of operation of the middle schools. It seemed that the first year would require many adjustments to a new organizational structure by students and staff. During the second year, a detailed plan was to be developed and then implemented in the third year, 1988.

Step 3: During the summer of 1987, four teams of teachers and administrators, one from each middle school, attended a week long middle school workshop at the University of Wisconsin—Platteville. This workshop focused on four aspects of an advisory program: logistics, in-service training, curriculum and resources, and communication/publicity. Other school personnel and various staff members attended different workshops and seminars during the planning phase.

Step 4: In the winter and spring of 1988 each of the schools sent 10 participants, including the building principals, to a two-day Trainer Workshop where they were trained by a consultant in facilitative skills and teacher advisor strategies. After experimenting with the skills in

> *...the first year would require many adjustments to a new organizational structure by students and staff.*

their schools in the interim, the participants met again one month later and learned how to co-lead eight inservice modules for teachers in their respective schools.

The training model was a modification of one used in Sarasota, Florida and Huntsville, Alabama (Myrick, Highland, & Highland, 1986). It provided an on-site inservice program, delivered by professional colleagues in the schools.

Step 5: Another subcommittee, working closely with the district guidance supervisor, developed three curriculum handbooks, one for each grade level (6, 7, and 8).

Step 6: OUR TIME was implemented in the fall of 1988.

What Were Some of the Initial Problems?

The biggest problem was teacher resistance. Some teachers complained that they were going to be "guidance counselors" and that this was not their job. The handbooks appeared to have too many written activities and there was a need for more hands-on activities. Some staff continued to see education as cognitive and felt uncomfortable with the idea of being responsible for affective education.

The biggest problem was teacher resistance.

The advisement concept was new to many teachers and they were unsure of their roles and skills. Some did not understand the philosophy and were concerned that advisory meetings would take away from teaching academics. And, there was some concern about preparation time needed for OUR TIME. There was an obvious need for staff understanding, support and training.

Parents were informed about the program through the newspaper, newsletters, and a mailed copy of a brochure. One parent asked to examine the curriculum and made some comments and recommendations about one of the guidance units. Otherwise, there has been no expression of parent resistance, only support.

There was an obvious need for staff understanding, support and training.

OUR TIME

OUR TIME is the name of the teacher advisory program in all four middle schools. The program is coordinated at the district level by the Supervisor of Guidance/Career

Education. At the school or building level, principals are the coordinators. In some cases they have asked a school counselor without an assigned advisory group to be responsible for coordination or to assist in some of the responsibilities. In one building, the assistant principal is the designated coordinator. Steering Committee members from each school continue to serve as liaisons and help in some of the coordinating duties.

Each middle school building has one principal and one assistant principal. One of the two administrators is assigned an advisory group. They may rotate by semesters or by the year. One is always available during OUR TIME for administrative business. As the instructional leaders in their buildings, these two administrators also provide ongoing leadership and support for the program.

Two of the three counselors in each middle school are assigned advisory groups. The third counselor is available to work with individual students needing assistance in crisis situations. This counselor also provides leadership and support for advisors and suggests helpful resources and techniques. All counselors periodically work with teachers regarding OUR TIME planning during weekly team meetings.

How Is the Program Scheduled?

The scheduling of OUR TIME during the school day proved to be a difficult issue. Although OUR TIME was recognized as an integral part of middle schools, it was necessary to negotiate its inclusion in the school schedule between the district administration and the teacher's bargaining unit, the Green Bay Education Association. It was finally agreed that the advisement groups would meet twice a week, Mondays and Thursdays, at the beginning of the school day. Each session would be 24 minutes, from 7:30 am to 7:54 am. The time was obtained by reducing the six regularly scheduled periods during the day by four minutes each.

After one year of experience with the program, it was decided to continue with the same time period twice a week but to meet on Wednesdays and Thursdays. These days are used for guidance activities. There is some discussion about the value and the logistics of expanding the program to five days a week, which would provide opportunities for such activities as sustained silent reading and individual conference time.

How Are Students and Advisors Matched?

All teachers in a middle school, except those who have split duty also in a high school, are assigned an advisory group. Other advisors include related arts teachers, two counselors, a librarian, and an administrator. The average number of students per group is about 15.

The middle schools are organized in "house" plans that consist of about 75 to 100 students and three to four teachers. This "family" is the base unit or bloc for meeting academic needs (e.g., reading, math, social studies, science, and language). Using a computer, students within a house and by grade level are randomly assigned to advisors. Attention is given to balancing the groups in terms of gender and behavior problems. The advisory groups remain together for one year.

One school administrator is always available to handle administrative duties. One of the three counselors in each school is not assigned a group and is available to deal with crisis situations, parents, and special assignments. This counselor also serves as a resource to advisors and assists with individual students.

Attention is given to balancing the groups in terms of gender and behavior problems.

Is There a Guidance Curriculum?

A curriculum guide was developed for each grade level (6–8) by a district committee of ten teachers and counselors. As one committee member said, "We borrowed appreciatively from many other generous school districts."

The goals of OUR TIME were outlined in a three-fold brochure which was distributed to parents and the community. The goals are:

- To emphasize the worth of the individual.
- To foster a school environment which develops a positive student-educator relationship.
- To recognize that each student possesses personal interests and needs.
- To direct each student according to his or her potential.

- To help each student develop a sense of self-direction.
- To help students solve school adjustment problems.
- To help each student explore career goals.
- To provide an experience in group dynamics.

These goals are further incorporated into curriculum topics such as orientation, study skills, friendships, stress management, peer pressure, conflict resolution and problem solving, leisure time, leadership, careers, and communication skills.

OUR TIME activities are put in three-ring binder notebooks and identified by grade level. Each activity is outlined in terms of objectives or related skills, materials needed, kind of groupings, and general procedures. An attempt was made to have at least eight to ten activities for each topic.

What Are an Advisor's Responsibilities?

The primary responsibility of an advisor is to become well-acquainted with each advisee and to develop a positive working relationship. The relationship should be perceived by the advisee as warm and caring in nature.

Advisors are charged with creating an atmosphere of "belonging" for their advisory groups, a place where students can feel accepted and where they can obtain help. Advisors also help their advisees learn more about themselves and others through guidance related activities (the curriculum).

Some students have more problems than others. When an advisee has needs which go beyond what a teacher-advisor can meet, advisors refer the case to school counselors.

How Did Teachers Respond to the Program?

Initially, teachers were concerned about the value of advisory groups and their roles in them. Throughout the first year, teachers' questions and concerns provided helpful feedback about the program and gave direction for modifications. As a result of teacher input, several helpful strategies were implemented, such as increased sharing among advisors through a newsletter, curriculum revisions, and special groups for students with problems. Time and experience have helped reduce concerns and worries.

Advisors are charged with creating an atmosphere of "belonging" for their advisory groups, a place where students can feel accepted....

As both students and teachers have become more familiar with the program, it has received more support. However, additional inservice training is still necessary. The curriculum is being reviewed and revised. There is a need for staff to share their successes and to explore their concerns. Some teachers have agreed to be videotaped and these tapes will be used for staff development.

Some teachers have agreed to be videotaped and these tapes will be used for staff development.

Special Features

One of the most important aspects of the program is that it has involved so many staff members. The training program in which a core of staff were prepared to be trainers of their colleagues proved to be a positive experience for both trainers and their teacher colleagues.

OUR TIME buttons with a unique logo were worn by staff to help announce the program. The name emphasized the goals of teacher advisement and provided a personal identity for the program.

An *OUR TIME Tip Sheet* is used in the district to communicate ideas among schools. It is a newsletter written by middle school advisors for middle school advisors. In one issue a goal-setting unit was described by an advisor in which students listed their goals at the beginning of the school year, sealed one copy in an envelope, and then opened that envelope at the end of the school year. Successes and failures were discussed in the advisory group.

Bulletin boards showing photos and sharing information about students is a popular activity in advisory groups. Collages that illustrate interests, hobbies, and future plans are also made.

Friendship bracelets were made in some groups and advisees studied careers through some board game activities, such as *Win, Lose or Draw* and the *Squeal of Fortune*. In one instance a sixth grade OUR TIME group was "kidnapped" by a seventh grade OUR TIME group. Then, the sixth graders were taken from their room to the seventh grade room where a problem solving mystery had been planned. Group interaction was observed and discussed. Doughnuts and juice were provided as an extra bonus for the day.

During the winter holiday season many of the OUR TIME groups incorporated the idea of "Secret Santas." The focus was not on buying gifts; rather, it was on sharing positive thoughts and doing good deeds for a fellow group member. In a special case, the mother of one student died. Group members responded by creating a sympathy card and writing a note to their friend. The advisor seized upon the moment to help students experience and learn more about being sensitive, caring, and supportive.

A building principal decided to have an advisory group. He was quoted in the local newspaper as saying, "I'm enjoying getting to know these kids on such a personal level....and they are getting to know that the principal is a person, too."

"OUR TIME is good for getting to know what is going on, to study our lives, and to free our minds from stress."

One student said, "OUR TIME is good for getting to know what is going on, to study our lives, and to free our minds from stress." Another commented, "You talk about your feelings and nobody can interrupt you. It is a program that helps you understand daily problems and deal with them." Still another student concluded, "OUR TIME is sort of like a talk show for teens, which deals with subjects that I think teens are interested in."

Looking Back and to the Future

Throughout the year, building principals and Steering Committee members at each school gather data from staff informally. A formal assessment was completed about midpoint and again at the end of the first year of implementation. Data were limited but showed general acceptance and support for the program. Advisors sought both informal and formal input from students at the completion of the different guidance units.

Teachers need more inservice. There are still sources of resistance which must be addressed. Follow-up staff development sessions, some with specific examples of advisors at work, will help.

The curriculum will continue to be modified and efforts will be made to identify more resource materials.

What Advice Do You Have for Those Who Are Starting?

Set aside time to plan the program before it starts. Two years of planning time is not unrealistic, as there are many issues which need to be addressed and it takes time to build a broad base of support.

A quality program requires adequate resources. Therefore, take account of the number of personnel who are available to be advisors, the materials that will be needed, and the cost to get the program started.

Select a good external consultant to provide staff training. Then, make provisions for local staff to follow-up with training and support. The consultant should be an effective facilitator as well as an expert on the topic, one who can help sell the idea to doubting teachers.

A carefully designed curriculum should be prepared by a committee representing the schools. This helps make the curriculum relevant to the community and stimulates a sense of ownership by the staff.

Steering committees are valuable in the planning and implementation of a program. They take the pressure off top-level administrators and provide a broader perspective from staff who are directly involved in the implementation of the program.

A quality program requires adequate resources.
...take account of the number of personnel... available..., the materials that will be needed, and the cost....

Chapter 5

TA Groups in LaPorte, Indiana

Charles Blair

Introduction

The LaPorte School Corporation serves the city of LaPorte, Indiana, population 24,000, as well as several smaller communities and rural areas encompassing 170 square miles in northwestern Indiana. The school corporation is committed to developmental guidance and counseling programs in all its schools. The teacher advisement program, called TA, was first introduced in the district's two middle schools (grades 6–8) in 1984. Each of the two middle schools has a student population of about 775, with professional faculty of 45, and this has held rather constant for the past decade. This kind of stability in the small rural area has made it possible to experiment with innovative educational programs.

Getting Started

Three factors led to the implementation of TAP. First, schools were facing a declining enrollment and there was a need to better utilize space. The decision to convert junior high schools to middle schools was based on economics as much as educational advantages. It was decided that if change was imminent then the schools should become exemplary and exemplify the true spirit of middle-level education and philosophy. Thus began a three-year study of middle school practices throughout the nation.

Second, dissatisfaction was growing with guidance programs in the junior high schools. The work of counselors

... counselors had no significant impact on students because their time was too often consumed by quasi-administrative tasks.

was being questioned; counselors had no significant impact on students because their time was too often consumed by quasi-administrative tasks. Not enough students were able to receive guidance and counseling services through the counseling staff alone.

Finally, new guidance and counseling programs were being developed and expanded at all levels in other places in the nation. In fact, elementary school counselors had been employed in LaPorte and their work with children demonstrated the value of students receiving activities which focused on their personal and social growth. Elsewhere, middle school counselors in exemplary schools complimented the work of teachers as advisors and, consequently, were able to work with more high-risk students. The developmental guidance model could positively affect student learning when it was implemented correctly.

What Were the First Steps to Getting Started?

Moving junior high schools to middle schools involved many organizational changes. New terms were introduced: assigning students to "houses" within the schools; team planning; block scheduling; exploratory classes; developmental guidance; and advisor/advisee programs. The changes also influence hiring and staff development practices.

Step 1: A steering committee to study middle schools, including guidance programs, was established in 1980.

Step 2: Visitations to other schools began in 1981 and were completed in 1982. Teachers in the two schools were divided into nine groups and these groups were responsible for studying various aspects of the schools they visited. Team reports were then submitted and studied. Twenty-two schools in five states were targeted for visits.

Step 3: The steering committee compiled all the data from the visitations and reviewed the professional literature. Recommendations were made to incorporate parts of programs from several schools and these were merged into a final plan. The most influential schools reflected in the plan were Spring Hill and Lincoln Middle Schools in Gainesville, Florida; Webster Transitional School in Cedarburg, Wisconsin; and the West Ottawa Middle School in Holland, Michigan.

Step 4: Inservice and staff development training took place during the 1983–84 school year.

Step 5: Public meetings were held periodically during the entire process over the four years. Teacher-parent conferences included information specific to TAP and a printed brochure was distributed to parents.

Step 6: The restructured middle schools, with advisor/advisee programs, opened in September of 1984. The transition was very smooth and parental complaints were non-existent during the year. Parental support still remains high.

What Were Some of the Initial Problems?

The new role of school counselors, which included classroom guidance and small group counseling, was a departure for both counselors and teachers. Teachers complained that they were doing the counselor's job as advisors in the advisor/advisee program. They said they were not trained to be counselors.

The resources and activity guidelines for teacher/advisors were limited at first. Many advisors were unsure of what to do and felt uncomfortable leading open discussions about topics which they felt unprepared to "teach." This mind-set related to traditional teaching methods hampered some teachers in making a quick adjustment.

Change usually arouses anxiety, regardless of what the change may be. This anxiety can feed upon itself and grow if not checked; unchecked, teacher anxiety can sabotage a program.

...unchecked, teacher anxiety can sabotage a program.

Advisory Group Meetings

The assistant superintendent for curriculum and instruction is responsible for elementary and middle school guidance programs at the district level. One counselor in each school is informally named as the contact person for the teacher advisor program (TA). There is no formal title or extra pay for this position.

How Is the Program Scheduled?

Both middle schools have TA twice a week. One has 30-minute sessions for all grade levels (6–8). The other school has 30 minutes for grade 6 but has 40 minutes for grades 7 and 8. On the remaining days the students have minicourses. All teachers are involved in TA and in minicourses.

The TA groups meet during the last period of the school day. Originally, they were held during the first period, but many teachers found they were spending too much time listening to students' problems from the evening or night before. Obviously, these problems were important but they kept TA from becoming a developmental program. This move from morning to afternoon seemed to make TA more workable and also fit with the schedule of minicourses.

How Are Students and Advisors Matched?

There are about 45 teachers in each school and all of them are assigned TA groups. Thus, the average size of a group ranges from 16 to 20 students. Counselors are not assigned groups, as they are expected to work with teachers and special groups of students during TA time.

In some years, the principals and counselors assigned groups to teachers. Currently, in both middle schools advisees are randomly matched with advisors. An effort is made to make sure the groups are balanced by separating all students into one of four student pools, based on boys/girls and academic achievement. Students are then evenly assigned to advisors from these four groups.

Groups are selected and matched to an advisor each school year. There is no carry-over of advisees to an advisor from year to year. This gives students an opportunity to build and expand new relationships. If a serious mismatch between advisor and advisee or within a group of students occurs, moving students to other groups might be done at the end of the semester; this rarely happens.

Is There a Guidance Curriculum?

In the beginning teachers were responsible for developing their own curricula. The guidance counselors and district staff compiled numerous group activities for teachers to use. In addition, they collected several curriculum guides from other schools and stored these in a central, accessible location for teachers. Since then, some commercially developed materials have been adopted for use.

The guidance curriculum for grade 6 for the first six weeks is called "Horizon" and it was developed by teachers and counselors in the local middle schools to be used in conjunction with an orientation mini-course called "Launch." For the remainder of the school year, topics vary from group to group according to the needs or interests of students. Teachers can draw upon a resource file of activities based on many topics. Focus on a particular topic may range in length of time from one week to six or nine weeks. The majority of topics deal with affective education. Other topics focus on such subjects as problem-solving, decision-making, keeping friends, and study skills.

Grade 7 uses the outline of the *Lions-Quest Skills for Adolescence Program*, adapting it to TA time periods and supplementing it with relevant topics selected by advisors.

The seven units, each with a distinct theme, are:

- Entering the Teen Years: The Challenge Ahead
- Building Self-confidence Through Better Communication
- Learning About Emotions: Developing Competence in Self-assessment and Self-discipline
- Friends: Improving Peer Relationships
- Strengthening Family Relationships
- Developing Critical-thinking Skills for Decision Making
- Setting Goals for Healthy Living

Each unit contains a wide variety of classroom activities which include discussion, assignments, guided practice in skills, and learning by offering service to others. All teachers and group leaders who offer the *Quest Program* are required to participate in a three-day training workshop sponsored by Quest International and the program materials are not available without this training.

The general curriculum guide for grade 8 is built around the *Degrassi Junior High Discussion and Activity Guide Program*, developed by WGBH Educational Foundation in Boston, Massachussetts as part of public broadcasting systems in the United States and Canada.

This program features episodes, taking place in an unnamed North American city, with a diversity of nationalities represented by students of Degrassi Junior High. The episodes portray real-life situations facing young

...topics focus on such subjects as problem-solving, decision-making, keeping friends, and study skills.

adolescents and focus on such issues as peer pressure, alcohol and drug abuse, child abuse, sexuality, body image, cultural values, social responsibility, and relationships. Although each one stands on its own, there is a storyline which threads its way through the series and finds some resolution in the final episodes. Cross themes also run through the series.

The use of the *Quest* and *Degrassi* programs relieved advisors in the 7th and 8th grades from searching for materials. Even though these programs offer a structured approach to guidance, choice and flexibility still remains with each TA group in terms of topics and activities.

Other activities are drawn from such books and resources as *Caring and Sharing* (Myrick & Erney, 1978); *Teacher as Facilitator* (Wittmer & Myrick, 1980) and peer facilitator materials which were given to all teachers. Books of selected activities are also available from school districts which were visited.

What Are the Advisor's Responsibilities?

The advisors are responsible for knowing their 16–20 advisees and working with them in their adjustment to school and personal, social, and academic growth. Advisory group meetings take place two times a week, which gives advisors an opportunity to have regular contact with students.

Advisors help identify students who need special attention and they are referred to counselors for more indepth guidance and counseling. Counselors, in turn, ask advisors to recommend students for small group counseling.

Advisors also act as student advocates and liaisons to their students' academic teams. Appropriate information is relayed by advisors to team members with the intent that a student's attitude, work habits, or learning situation may be improved.

Advisors also act as student advocates and liaisons to their students' academic team.

How Did Teachers Respond to the Program?

Initially, perhaps only 15 percent of the teachers either strongly supported or generally supported the TA program. At least 5 percent were strongly opposed. Thus, about 80 percent were undecided but willing to go along, or did not generally support the idea. However, support is currently running as high as 70 percent, with about 30 percent still undecided or resistant.

The teachers who do not support the program argue that it takes time which could be devoted to academics and they feel uncomfortable with the advisor's role, especially leading group guidance sessions. At first, many teachers resisted by saying they were not counselors nor did they intend to do what counselors should be doing. However, over the years this complaint has disappeared, especially as counselor and advisor roles were clarified and as counselors became more active in small group counseling with targeted students. There is now a better understanding of how their roles complement one another. A few teachers have never bought into the program. Although their number is small, they are often vocal. As support from the mainstream of teachers has grown, peer pressure has kept the resistant teachers from organizing an effective effort against the program. Even though they basically oppose it, they also go along with the program and some do a very effective job. Because teachers were not given a choice of whether or not they wanted to participate, some were swept up in the enthusiastic response by their colleagues and students. Middle school principals helped by taking a strong stand in support of TA.

...support is currently running as high as 70 percent, with about 30 percent still undecided or resistant.

Middle school principals helped by taking a strong stand in support of TA.

Looking Back and to the Future

How Do You Evaluate TA?

Some attempts have been made to informally evaluate the activities and guidance units in TA. Surveys showed that most students and teachers are supportive of the program and that it is becoming an integral part of the school. The district contracted for more formal evaluative procedures with an external evaluator from Ball State University.

The middle school guidance and counseling program as a whole has been extensively studied and evaluated. The results of these studies have validated the developmental model, including the value of emphasizing large and small group guidance.

Perhaps the greatest strength of the TA program is its inclusiveness. The program can be adapted to meet the needs of individuals and groups. The idea that a student is just a number or a nonentity going through school is antithetical to the program. Students need advocates, people who care and who are interested in their progress. The advisory program is the only logical way in which individuals can receive special attention in schools with hundreds of students. Giving this attention is a major goal of TA in LaPorte.

What Key Factors Have Contributed to the Program's Success?

It helped to draw upon the commitment and knowledge of principals and assistant principals who had elementary school experience. They sensed the value of a developmental guidance program and were eager to implement the idea. These administrators participated willingly in inservice meetings, where they learned more about TA and the advisor skills needed to make it work.

School counselors also played an important role. They had participated in several inservice workshops prior to the restructuring of the middle schools. They became more skilled and their perspective about the work of the counselor was broadened. They saw themselves doing more group work. The retrained and renewed counselors provided administrators an additional set of helpers who could assist in the transition. Some teachers were impressed with the new attitudes and strategies used by the counselors. The transformation helped teachers to see that change, although difficult, could be accomplished and that it was both professionally and personally rewarding. Change was not any easier for counselors than teachers, but as teachers saw counselors in a different light there was an increased readiness for accepting the change.

In the beginning, counselors met with parents of incoming 5th and 6th graders from elementary schools. Parents were fearful that their children were going to school with "big kids" and that they would be lost in the shuffle of things. After hearing about the middle school and TA, parents were encouraging and supportive. Not one negative call was received from any parent.

Counselors consulted with teachers about TA and helped put together sets of activities, books, and guidance units. They placed appropriate resource materials in a room near

> *...as teachers saw counselors in a different light there was an increased readiness for accepting the change.*

their offices and talked with teachers about their concerns and interests. Perhaps the single most important contribution to the guidance curriculum was the addition of more structure through *Quest* and *Degrassi* activities.

If students like the school and TA, then parents' apprehensions, if any, are going to disappear; this is also true for teachers. Administrators, counselors and teachers were prepared to get off to a good start with students and they did. Subsequent modifications and revisions came as a result from everyone in the school being involved in the program.

One may hope that the rationale and philosophy of the program, coupled with the potential outcomes, would be enough to sell the program to teachers. But, typical of most schools in the nation, initial teacher resistance and skepticism ran high. Some people simply approach change more enthusiastically and positively than others. Some reluctant individuals may find it difficult to say anything positive.

A turning point for some teachers came when building principals took a strong stand and said that all teachers would be advisors. Moreover, principals announced that TA was going to be an outstanding program and there would be no alibis, no excuses, no complaining. Rather than continue to listen to skeptics or nonsupporters, the principals dismissed their complaints and said, in essence, "Just do it." Without any recourse, some of the most resistant teachers turned to the task of making TA work and many of them later became the staunchest supporters of the program after they began participating. For whatever reason, some people simply need to know that there is no choice and that they are expected to respond to the challenge. And, they do.

If students like the school and TA, then parents' apprehensions... are going to disappear....

A turning point for some teachers came when building principals took a strong stand and said that all teachers would be advisors.

What Advice Do You Have for Those Who Are Starting?

Considerable planning went into the restructuring of the schools and the implementation of TA. Careful planning and involvement of as many administrators, teachers, and parents as possible can set the tone for change.

However, change is a lot like the vaudevillian who takes sticks and spins plates on them. If they wobble, then they must be spun again. You have to respin some parts in a changing school or program. Some parts wobble more than others, especially when there are no words of praise.

It takes time for people to orient themselves to new approaches. They might try out small segments with students at first and then make revisions. With experience and success, they try to do more and take more risks.

While group guidance is the backbone of TA, counseling is still a central part of meeting middle school student needs. School counselors must be trained and they must establish their own identity and program, with a special emphasis on small group counseling. Teachers want to know that counselors are pulling their fair share of the guidance and counseling load.

All activities in TA need to be evaluated, even if it is only a three-question "yes/no" format. Make sure that students understand the value of evaluating a guidance unit and how to complete evaluation forms. Pre-post data is not always easy to assess because some students rate themselves too high on desired behaviors in the beginning, before they are familiar with the concepts on the evaluation instrument. For example, students might rate themselves as good listeners on a pre-test, only to learn through TA group activities that their listening skills were more limited than they realized. Outside school evaluators are helpful and they can provide objectivity.

One problem LaPorte is encountering is both teacher and administrator turnover. If turnover is rapid, then history, continuity, and perspective can be lost. New teachers and administrators need to study and review the program as part of their pre-service orientation.

Finally, on-going staff development renews enthusiasm and support, especially when it comes from outside resources.

Visitations to model schools or exemplary programs, sharing ideas with others, practicing new skills, and trying out new strategies for helping students are productive ways to encourage a faculty to maintain a successful program.

New teachers and administrators need to study and review the program as part of their pre-service orientation.

Chapter 6

The Middle School Advisory Program in the Collegiate Schools, Richmond, Virginia

Sally Chambers

Introduction

Teacher advisor programs have proven successful in private as well as public schools. The Collegiate Schools (grades K–12) in Richmond, Virginia is the second largest independent day school on the east coast of the United States with an enrollment of about 1300 students. Although a homeroom system in the former girls school and an advisor system in the former boys school have been in place for several years, a more structured approach, the Advisory Program, was incorporated into the daily schedule.

Teacher advisor programs have proven successful in private as well as public schools.

Getting Started

As part of a restructuring plan for the total school, implemented in 1986, it was decided to continue with a coed Lower School (K–4) and to create a coordinate Middle School (5–8) and a coed Upper School (9–12). This meant that girls and boys at the middle school level would be housed in the same building but academic subjects would be grouped by single sex classes. Many exploratory classes, however, would become coeducational.

A Middle School Guidance Task Force, composed of eight faculty members teaching in the middle grades and the school counselor, was a part of the restructuring process. The Task Force examined the total guidance program, including student advisement. A study of the existing

> *The faculty agreed to involve more teachers in an advisory role, creating a student-faculty ratio of 1–15.*

advisory systems showed some teachers to be overloaded in coordinating progress reports and report cards for about 50 students. Advisors focused primarily on academic progress of individual students. The faculty agreed to involve more teachers in an advisory role, creating a student-faculty ratio of 1–15. This allowed more faculty to share the responsibility for routine academic and clerical tasks and also created more opportunities to promote closer faculty/student relationships.

What Were the First Steps in Getting Started?

Step 1: The task force studied the guidance needs and issues in the school and presented a rationale for the Advisory Program based on (1) the value of recognizing preadolescent developmental stages; (2) the need for an appropriate transitional program to bridge the lower and upper schools; and, (3) the importance of developing positive self-concepts and a sense of compassion for others.

Step 2: Parents were informed about the program through a parent newsletter and then in parent-led discussion groups. The program was discussed in detail at grade-level curriculum meetings, which were attended by faculty and parents. Finally, as part of preparation, the program was described by advisors at Patrons' Night, an annual "back-to-school" meeting.

Step 3: Recognizing that the middle school faculty would be dealing with many new roles in a restructured school, the administration decided that the Advisory Program would be implemented over two years. During the first year, the program was put into the schedule and students were divided into single-sex groupings of approximately 15–20 students. Groups met for about 30 minutes daily and followed this schedule:

Monday:	Advisory Group Meetings
Tuesday:	Assembly or Chapel Programs
Wednesday:	Club Meetings
Thursday:	Class Meetings/Advisory Group Meetings
Friday:	Schoolwide silent reading

This structure allowed teachers and advisees to get to know each other better by meeting and working together informally. Communication with parents and other faculty members was a primary goal of advisors. They coordinated parent conferences and became more familiar with student records and reports. Advisors were not expected to lead "affective education activities" in the first year.

Step 4: A two-day training workshop was arranged for advisors as part of the preschool fall planning period. This workshop focused on helping advisors to create more positive working relationships with students and to lead guidance activities with their advisees. Thus, in the second year advisors were expected to expand their responsibilities, including the implementation of guidance curriculum through structured group activities. The experiential workshop helped set the tone for the program, and participants came to know each other better because of shared experiences.

Step 5: The guidance curriculum for the Advisory Program was first designed by the school counselor, who drew upon resources from other schools and books of structured activities. This first set of activities, based around common themes, provided teachers a resource book and gave some organization to the program.

Step 6: Students were prepared for the Advisory Program by the advisors themselves. Goals were stated and clarified. The program was then implemented.

What Were Some of the Initial Problems?

The school was being restructured, which meant the faculty was under extra stress even though the restructuring was generally approved and everyone was hopeful about the changes. There was some initial skepticism about the role of advisors and how much extra preparation was needed to prepare for advisory group meetings. Some faculty were uneasy about leading guidance discussions and did not like the idea of following a curriculum guide. Some lacked self-confidence and were unsure of their role as an advisor.

Some faculty were uneasy about leading guidance discussions and did not like the idea of following a curriculum guide.

The Advisory Program

The Advisory Program is coordinated by the school counselor, who was also given the responsibility for developing the initial guidance curriculum. The counselor helped

The counselor, as coordinator, helps teachers identify appropriate group activities....

arrange for staff development workshops, consulted with administrators and teachers regarding the program, and met with parents who had particular concerns or interests. The counselor, as coordinator, helps teachers identify appropriate group activities for Mondays and Thursdays and assists advisors in meeting advisees' special needs and interests. Two Lead Advisors, one for boys and one for girls, at each grade level work with the counselor in coordinating the curriculum. The other days—assemblies/chapels, clubs, silent reading—are coordinated by the administration.

How Is the Program Scheduled?

There are eight periods in a school day which runs from 8:10 a.m. until 3:20 p.m., with a 26-minute lunch period. The Advisory Program is scheduled for 33 minutes each day from 9:44 to 10:17 a.m. Advisors believe that this midmorning break is timely in a challenging academic day.

Group guidance activities are scheduled for Mondays and Thursdays. On some occasions, class meetings are held on Thursdays. This is a time when the boys and the girls at a grade level meet separately for class projects led by class officers. Assemblies or chapel programs take place on Tuesdays. On Wednesdays students choose from a range of club meetings (e.g., computer, drama, chorus, literary magazine) or remain in their Advisory Group for informal advisement or socializing. Elected student representatives from each advisory group attend student government meetings. This time is used by some students to see other teachers for tutorial help.

On Fridays everyone in the school, including advisors and administrators, read silently during this period. Students are encouraged to read a book or magazine for enjoyment rather than one assigned by a teacher.

How Are Students and Advisors Matched?

At the end of the academic year the advisors make recommendations to the administration for next year's groupings. Attempts are made to create heterogeneous single-sex groups of academic ability, personality traits, and special interests. Consideration is also given to compatibility of students and equal responsibilities among advisors. The

Middle School typically has three advisory groups of boys and three of girls at each grade level.

The middle school has a pool of 29 potential advisors, which does not include shared or part-time faculty, secretaries or administrators; 23 teachers function as advisors, working with approximately 400 students in groups of about 15 students each.

Is There a Guidance Curriculum?

The guidance curriculum for the Advisory Program is focused on the time when advisors lead group activities. It is divided into six thematic areas, one each for six grading periods during the school year. The themes are:

1. Becoming oriented to the Middle School and Advisory Group—Enhancing self-awareness.
2. Exploring choices and values—Decision-making skills.
3. Improving communication skills.
4. Exploring group dynamics.
5. Appreciating positive peer relationships.
6. Appreciating positive family relationships.

Advisors are encouraged to plan and lead at least six group activities from the thematic areas each grading period. In addition, a drug education curriculum is available and includes the six basic themes.

An Advisory Handbook of suggested activities was given to each advisor as a place to start. One handbook was created for fifth and sixth grade advisors and another handbook for seventh and eighth grades. As advisors discovered new activities for the theme areas, they copied and inserted them into the handbooks as resources to draw upon. Efforts are being made to create enough activities that they need not be repeated from a previous year or grade level.

What Are an Advisor's Responsibilities?

The Middle School Advisor in the Collegiate Schools has six responsibilities:

1. To know each advisee on a personal basis, probably better than most other faculty members.
2. To build group cohesiveness in the Advisory Group.

3. To lead structured affective education activities.
4. To coordinate communication among faculty and parents about student needs and progress.
5. To manage the distribution and collection of progress reports and report cards for advisees.
6. To seek out assistance for students with special needs and to make appropriate referrals.

How Did Teachers Respond to the Program?

The most favorable response came from fifth and sixth grade advisors, who were initially enthusiastic and provided very strong support for the program, including the group activities.

The seventh and eighth grade advisors were generally supportive but there was more variance, especially in terms of leading "affective education activities" and following a prescribed curriculum.

Some favorable comments by fifth and sixth grade advisors were:

> ➤ "It provides an opportunity for a teacher to get to know students in a different way."
> ➤ "The Advisory Program provides a homebase of support for hurts, disappointments, and joys."
> ➤ "The Advisory Program provides a structured, yet flexible forum for students to discuss concerns, ideas, and problems."
> ➤ "Students need to have a person outside classes, who they know cares and will listen."
> ➤ "The group gives students a 'home'...a school family."

Comments by the seventh and eighth grade advisors regarding the program's strengths included the following:

> ➤ "It provides students an advocate at school."
> ➤ "The program helps students learn to monitor their own behavior and to become more responsible."
> ➤ "The Advisory Program is a place to 'put out fires.'"
> ➤ "The Advisory Program creates a group that works, plays, and learns from each other."
> ➤ "It encourages good communication among students, faculty, and parents."

"The Advisory Program provides a structured, yet flexible forum for students to discuss concerns, ideas, and problems."

Special Features

The daily contact of advisors and advisees in both formal and informal discussions has enabled people in the school to know each other better. The cohesiveness of the advisory groups was best illustrated when some students and advisors said that they wanted to remain as a group in the coming year. However, all students are assigned to new advisors and groups each year. One feature of the program is an emphasis on service to the school and community. At the time of nationally recognized holidays, caring and sharing are emphasized. Concern for those in less fortunate positions is expressed through organized activities in advisory groups such as adoption of a family for assistance, making gifts, special dinners, and holiday decorations. Advisory groups also assume different school tasks, such as flag duty, maintenance of the school building, and service projects.

During each grading period advisors work with the school counselor to identify students who are deserving of special recognition for a particular achievement. This might include demonstrating a positive school attitude, helping others at school, promoting school spirit, excelling in music or fine arts, or demonstrating effort at academic improvement. Advisors look for ways to help all their advisees obtain some kind of special recognition during the school year, which is celebrated through periodic ice cream sundae making parties.

On Conference Day students do not come to school. Advisors and parents use the day to meet and communicate about students. The focus is on the interests, needs, and special circumstances affecting students. This is different from Patron's Night, when parents follow their children's schedules and learn more about the school curriculum. Advisors are prepared with input from the faculty who teach each student and this information can be shared if and when appropriate. But, the meetings are aimed primarily at building a cooperative working relationship between school and home.

One feature of the program is an emphasis on service to the school and community.

Looking Back and to the Future

Formal evaluation of advisors is the responsibility of the administration of the middle school. Advisors are asked to complete self-evaluation forms in the spring of the year and they are discussed in individual conferences with the Head of the Middle School, who talks about strengths and areas which might need improvement.

The Lead Advisors meet about four times a year to assess the overall progress of the Advisory Program. They share their ideas and impressions, meeting with the counselor in an ongoing dialogue. Parent and student evaluations are obtained informally and each advisor is responsible for obtaining informal feedback from his or her advisees.

What Key Factors Have Contributed to the Program's Success?

Advisors who genuinely care about their advisees have made the difference in the program. From the beginning most of the advisors had open minds....

Advisors who genuinely care about their advisees have made the difference in the program. From the beginning most of the advisors had open minds and a willingness to learn new roles in order to make the school a better place to be. Some teachers had already been highly effective in communicating with students and these teachers provided good role models for others. The former homeroom and advisor programs were not as systematic or as comprehensive, but they did provide teachers an opportunity to become familiar with some of the advisor-advisee concepts prior to the initiation of the Advisory Program.

The school administration believed in the worth of the program and understood the rationale behind it. Administrators used numerous opportunities to talk about the link between achievement, an outstanding middle school, and a strong Advisory Program. Besides general support, the administration made it clear that the Advisory Program was a high priority by the way in which new teachers were interviewed and employed. It was not enough to be an effective teacher, one had to also be an effective advisor.

...support and enthusiasm for the program will grow over time....

Teacher preparation is most important. Specific skills exist which help advisors to be good helpers and effective group leaders. Roles and skills must be identified and clarified. One should not expect that initially all teachers will support the program. Some teachers will be skeptical and some will lack self-confidence in leading group guidance sessions. However, support and enthusiasm for the program will grow over time, especially as advisors see and hear about positive outcomes.

Most faculty members are feeling more at ease with their advisor roles and becoming more comfortable in leading group guidance sessions. They are gaining more confidence in relating with their advisees and are becoming more sensitive to their needs. However, some faculty members still have difficulty breaking away from traditional teaching roles and methods. They resist the idea of leading guidance activities, perhaps unsure of what to expect or feeling out of control.

Some advisors questioned the validity and age-appropriateness of a few suggested activities in their handbooks. Some of the activities seem to them to be artificial or too contrived and they would prefer to have an open discussion with students about their interests rather than follow a curriculum. In most cases, this is not a major problem since Advisors must use their best judgement about the appropriateness of an activity. Some activities might well be questioned since they are still being studied, tested, and modified for use in group discussions.

A few advisors say that students do not like the activities, claiming they are too juvenile or too much like schoolwork. Almost always it is the way in which an advisor presents an activity and then leads the discussion which affects student attitudes and behaviors. Some students reflect their advisor's resistant attitude and lack of enthusiasm. Some uncertainty continues about how to go about turning around the attitudes of the doubting teachers and make them feel more positive about the program.

Additional staff development and training is probably the most important need in order to continue the development of a strong advisory program. A need still exists to help advisors learn more about group dynamics and leading guidance activities.

Being able to see the positive outcomes of a strong program has been very reinforcing for advisors. The faculty talked about knowing students better than ever before and being more aware of what students are interested in learning as well as what their problems are. The program provided a time when students could learn about themselves and others, without taking time away from academic studies. More communication is taking place between school and homes, and parents say that the school is more responsive to their children's needs. The faculty feels more like a team working

Additional staff development and training is probably the most important need in order to continue the development of a strong advisory program.

together, as they share more responsibilities and work cooperatively to help students. Successful experiences tend to breed further success.

What Advice Do You Have for Those Who Are Starting?

Faculty support prior to implementing an Advisory Program is essential. Teachers need to be involved from the beginning and during the initial planning stages. They need to believe that it is their program and that it is a valid part of what the school is offering.

Poor planning and lack of attention to logistics in the beginning will confuse the faculty and start negative thinking. Daily contact between advisors and advisees is essential and should be scheduled accordingly. Efforts should be made to make sure that this time is consistent and interference should be the exception rather than the rule. The focus should be on developmental guidance activities one or two days a week, giving all students more opportunities to learn about themselves and others.

Daily contact between advisors and advisees is essential and should be scheduled accordingly.

Chapter 7

TAP in Pasco County, Florida

Madonna Wise
Cathy Micheau

Introduction

Pasco County is located on Florida's Gulf Coast, north of the Tampa Bay and St. Petersburg/Clearwater communities. The Pasco County School District, 14th largest in the state, has over 31,000 students enrolled in 40 schools.

Teacher advisor programs are featured in both middle and high schools in the Pasco County Schools in Florida. The middle school advisement plan is called The Personal Enrichment Program (PEP) and is operating in six schools. Middle schools were the first to have teacher advisement programs and set an example for high schools. It is the development of the high school Teacher Advisor Program which will be discussed here.

The high school program is referred to as Teacher Advisor Program (TAP) and is currently in four of the county's six high schools. While programs may vary from one school to another in order to accommodate schedules, different school populations, and teacher interests, advisement programs share a common foundation. Advisement programs are based on the principles of developmental psychology/guidance. Program activities focus on major developmental tasks such as academic success, career exploration, decision-making, and interpersonal efficacy. The TAP plan was developed during the 1984–85 school year. It was first introduced into Pasco Comprehensive High School (Grades 9–12) as a pilot program. Three additional high schools have since implemented TAP: Ridgewood High

Advisement programs are based on the principles of developmental psychology/guidance

School, Gulf Comprehensive High School, and Hudson High School. A fifth high school, Land O' Lakes High School, received a Florida Department of Education grant in June of 1989 and plans are being made to implement TAP in 1990.

Getting Started

Several factors contributed to the school district's interest in TAP. Educators were concerned about the problems facing young people and these problems were directly related to progress in school. The Florida schools had a high dropout rate. In addition, educators were being asked to help prevent academic failure, teen pregnancy, drug abuse, and juvenile delinquency. The state legislators had increased graduation requirements in Florida high schools and there was a greater need to support students as they faced these additional pressures.

As a result, the first pilot program at Pasco Comprehensive High School focused on "at-risk" students. Special attention was given to minority students, alternative education students, and exceptional education students who were in danger of dropping out of school. Students were asked to participate voluntarily and to meet with teachers who were designated as special advisors. The program was expanded the following year to serve all students in the school.

The assumption behind high school TAP is the same as that for middle schools. A need exists for an organized advisement program where a caring adult is linked with a group of students as their advisor. The advisor is an information disseminator, a friendly listener, and a student advocate.

What Were the First Steps to Getting Started?

Step 1: District-level Student Services administrators noted the success of the advisement program (PEP) in the middle schools and believed that such a program would also be valuable in the high schools. A planning committee was organized to study the potential for high school advisory groups. The committee reviewed materials from other schools (e.g., Ferguson-Florissant Schools in Missouri; Cobb County Schools in Georgia; Wilde Lake High School in Maryland). Financial support for high school advisement came from the Florida Legislature and Department of Education in the form of the Omnibus Education Act (1984) which provided grant money to pilot TAP sites.

Step 2: A steering committee within the high school was organized to consider the information and recommendations of the initial planning committee. This committee surveyed faculty members and also developed a visitation form which was used by various faculty members who visited other schools with advisement programs. This provided some uniformity in observations and data collection.

The committee also examined the student advisement services already available in the school through school counselors, occupational specialists, and the career education program.

Step 3: District administrators wrote a DOE grant proposal for the implementation of TAP, which was funded. These funds provided for a TAP Coordinator and a TAP secretary. The TAP Coordinator took responsibility for providing leadership to the program and developing a series of guidance units which could be used by advisors.

Step 4: State funds were also used to provide staff development training to teachers at the high school. Inservice workshops were arranged on Saturdays for interested faculty and a week-long workshop was offered in the summer. Participants were paid a stipend for attending.

Step 5: The district guidance supervisor and the TAP coordinator continued to provide timely inservice training and consultation throughout the school year. Voluntary training sessions, conducted by the Coordinator during the year, focused on "how to" strategies for facilitating group meetings with advisees.

Step 6: Parents received introductory letters about TAP. Open house programs included a demonstration of TAP activities.

Step 7: TAP was first implemented in January of 1985, after about five months of planning and program development activities.

Parents received introductory letters about TAP.

Teacher resistance was a critical issue. Approximately 25 percent of the teachers had serious concerns....

What Were Some of the Initial Problems?

Barriers facing the implementation of TAP were not unlike those which might accompany any significant change in a school setting. Teacher resistance was a critical issue.

Approximately 25 percent of the teachers had serious concerns about TAP and there were others who were less than supportive. They were apprehensive about being placed in a group facilitator role and some were unsure that they were qualified to be advisors. "I can't do this...I wasn't trained to be a counselor," said one teacher. However, most of the teachers were assisted greatly through staff development training and the competence and role issues were less intense.

Teachers were also concerned about the amount of time that would be required for advisement and record keeping and they wondered about compensation for an extra preparation. The latter was eventually addressed and resolved through the district's bargaining unit and teacher contracts.

Another barrier in the first year of TAP was the reluctance of seniors in the school to support the program. Seniors were less responsive than students in grades 9–11 and their resistance tended to dampen enthusiasm for the program. Advisors had to work hard to involve them. With exposure to TAP, succeeding senior classes have been more receptive and student resistance is no longer a serious problem.

A problem also existed about how to make TAP meeting times a priority during the school week. The initial infrequency of TAP meetings—about once every two weeks—caused the bonding between advisor and advisee to bog down; there was not enough continuity. Again, staff development training helped correct the problem. More time was scheduled for advisement in subsequent years and on a more regular basis.

Parent resistance was nearly nonexistent. Any concerns expressed by parents seemed to be addressed when they received specific information about the purposes and goals of TAP through letters and at school meetings. A few phone calls came from people who were concerned about "delving into children's personal and social lives." Some school administrators thought that a fundamentalist faction in the community might raise objections to some of the proposed advisory activities, but this did not prove to be an issue.

TAP

From the beginning, guidance staff were involved in the organization of TAP. The program was initiated by the district's guidance supervisor and it is under the umbrella of developmental guidance.

The school guidance counselors have many roles in TAP, including: information resource, program troubleshooter, counseling referral source, and teacher consultant/trainer. Counselors are actively and visibly involved in TAP. They circulate among TAP groups during TAP meeting times. They coordinate guest speakers for TAP sessions and, on occasion, serve as guest speakers themselves. They conduct staff development activities for TAP and serve on TAP cluster support teams. At least one counselor is a member of each school's TAP steering committee, helping the committee to plan activities which reflect the school's current guidance themes.

Counselors are actively and visibly involved in TAP.

Steering committees are composed of 5–12 members who meet on a regular basis, usually weekly. Membership includes teachers, counselors, administrators, and at least one student representative. The committee provides program administration and leadership.

State funds are no longer available to hire a school-based coordinator and secretary for TAP as they were during the first year. Therefore, all TAP programs in the district are now coordinated by the steering committees and guidance staff in their respective schools. The program is coordinated at the district level by the Supervisor of Student Services.

The principal has the following roles in TAP:

1. Serves on the TAP steering committee and helps prioritize activities.
2. Arranges the TAP group meeting schedule.
3. Circulates throughout the school during TAP time and on occasion is a guest speaker.
4. Monitors and assesses the program.
5. Serves on a grade-level TAP support team.

How Is the Program Scheduled?

Currently, teacher advisor groups are scheduled to meet a minimum of once a week for 35 minutes. TAP is included in an activity bell schedule in which a few minutes are taken from each regularly scheduled class period during the day in order to create the meeting time within the school day.

TAP has generally been scheduled in the morning, usually after second period. Attempts have been made to vary the meeting times throughout the school day, but it was found that afternoon advisement time conflicted with student release for the vocational center and work release programs.

Advisement sessions are scheduled every day for the first two weeks of school. Advisors focus on orientation, review of the school's handbook, code of student conduct, school procedures, study skills, and self-concept related to school. Additional sessions are scheduled when it is time to distribute report cards and to register students for the next school year. Individual advisement sessions for advisees are required at least one time per semester and usually once during each six-week grading period. On some occasions, advisors meet individually with advisees when "back up" advisors are available to meet with the other advisors in their groups.

Advisors are required to talk with their advisees' parents at least one time per semester. This parent contact is considered essential to both the value of TAP and good public relations.

> ...parent contact is considered essential to both the value of TAP and good public relations.

How Are Students and Advisors Matched?

Assignments of advisees to advisors is made on a random basis and advisory groups are formed on the basis of grade level. All students are included in the random grouping, including those in ESE (Exceptional Student Education) and alternative education programs.

All TAP programs in the district have adopted the philosophy that it is most beneficial for advisees to stay with their advisors for their four years of high school. Accordingly, an advisee would move through grades 9–12 with the same advisor. Some exceptions to this guideline occur to facilitate programmatic logistics, as well as interpersonal conflicts between advisors and advisees. When such a change is indicated, a counselor meets with those involved to facilitate the process.

> ...it is most beneficial for advisees to stay with their advisors for their four years of high school.

Teacher participation as advisors varies from school to school and this, in turn, affects advisor/advisee ratios. The percentage of teacher involvement and respective ratios are shown below:

School	Percent of Teachers Involved	Ratio of Students Per Group
Pasco Comp.	78	30:1
Ridgewood	98	25:1
Gulf Comp.	100	20:1
Hudson	80	25:1

TAP is considered a legitimate curriculum assignment under the Pasco USEP employee's contract. As much as possible, teachers are asked to volunteer to be advisors and to participate in the program.

Is There a Guidance Curriculum?

To help advisors implement a developmental guidance program, seven TAP modules were designed as part of the curriculum. These modules are:

1. Orientation to TAP
2. Enhancing Motivation
3. Facilitative Communication
4. Decision-making and problem-solving
5. Interpreting and understanding school records and test results
6. Career advisement
7. Academic advisement

Each of the modules are contained in separate spiral binder books and were developed by the first year's TAP coordinator. A few general ideas and concepts on the topic of the module are presented in each book. Next, some structured learning activities are outlined: title, goal, objective, materials, and procedures. Advisors use the modules and activities as a resource for working with their advisees in any way that they may choose. In general, advisors tend to follow the order of the seven modules listed above.

Copies of all seven TAP modules are available to advisors. A TAP recordkeeping file box and folder for each advisee is also given to them. Other resources included are referral information lists, career pamphlets, and numerous brochures and pamphlets related to pertinent issues such as study skills and time management.

As new information or relevant resources become available, such as magazine articles and books, they are shared with advisors.

What Are the Advisor's Responsibilities?

Each high school advisor is seen as a group facilitator of the weekly TAP group sessions. Although some teachers are hesitant to lead group guidance sessions, this responsibility is usually critical to expanding a program and providing more developmental guidance services to all students.

Advisors must meet individually with advisees, no less than one time per semester. Likewise, parental contacts are made at least once a semester.

Some routine guidance tasks are also the responsibility of advisors, such as the distribution of progress reports and report cards. In this case, the advisor's main contribution is in follow up sessions related to the reports.

How Did Teachers Respond to the Program?

Teachers responded differently. Anxiety was high in some instances, as teachers were unsure and the program was unfamiliar to them. Some misunderstood the rationale for TAP and could not explain it. Others simply preferred to invest more time in their academic subject and saw TAP as an intrusion on teaching academics. Even some of those who were considered effective classroom teachers were hesitant about leading group guidance sessions.

Still other teachers responded enthusiastically. They welcomed the opportunity to meet students on a more personal basis. Many of them were convinced that students would like school better because of TAP and that improved academic performance would be related to the effectiveness of TAP. A great deal of skepticism dissipated as teachers had an opportunity to discuss ideas and work together in the staff development workshops. The information and training in skills improved teacher attitudes towards TAP.

A great deal of skepticism dissipated as teachers had an opportunity to discuss ideas and work together....

Special Features

Beginning with Pasco Comprehensive High School, the district has been awarded five TAP grants from the Florida Department of Education. Success is building upon success and each new TAP program seems to be more comprehensive than those which preceeded it. It is the goal of the district to have TAP in all six high schools by 1991.

Some of the schools have a half-time or full-time TAP coordinator, who assists advisors to assemble materials or prepare for group advisory meetings. The coordinator is also available to follow up on requests for information or perhaps to coordinate some special assistance for individual students.

The TAP materials were selected from many sources and were organized into the seven modules (handbooks). These have proven helpful to advisors, as they may select activities which appeal to them. As TAP expands and includes additional group guidance days, there will be a need to examine the modules and to consider what other themes and activities might be added.

Guest speakers from the community often speak during TAP period. This helps bridge the gap between school and community and draws on valuable resources.

Looking Back and to the Future

Since TAP was initially funded by the Florida DOE, evaluation and status reports were routine. Structured interviews and self-audits showed that teachers were generally supportive of advisement and that they believed in the concepts and rationale of the program. They made suggestions for changes in scheduling and recordkeeping, and teachers appreciated the opportunity to assess the program and make recommendations.

Over the years some positive changes have taken place because of TAP. Improvement in school attendance by students was dramatic during the first quarter of TAP's implementation at Pasco Comprehensive High School. There has also been an increase in the number/percentage of

Improvement in school attendance by students was dramatic during the first quarter of TAP's implementation....

students entering colleges/universities. These outcomes related to TAP have reinforced advisors and inspired others to want TAP in their schools.

What Key Factors Have Contributed to the Program's Success?

Above all else, principal support of TAP has been the key issue.

Above all else, principal support of TAP has been the key issue. Without administrative interest and support it would not have been possible to even initiate the first steps. Administrative vision, leadership, and commitment at the district level has been invaluable.

Careful planning makes a difference. Although Pasco County benefited from state grants, the foundation for a developmental guidance program through TAP was already being laid by PEP in the middle schools. Guidance and counseling via special student services was moving ahead with positive results and it was relatively easy to fit TAP into the scope of existing services. TAP made it possible to reach more students, to be more flexible, and to address more skills and objectives.

TAP made it possible to reach more students, to be more flexible, and to address more skills and objectives.

It was helpful to have school-based TAP advisors consult with, visit, and observe TAP programs in other Florida school districts. This stimulated their thinking and provided a reality base for concepts and logistical procedures.

Providing high quality and frequent staff development opportunities was very critical to program efficacy. Both internal and external consultants play significant roles in preparing the faculties for TAP. These consultants also helped set the tone for implementation, acknowledging that everyone was involved in a "process of learning, experimenting, and growing" rather than receiving a "canned" guidance program. It was important for teachers to listen, share ideas, and be open to change.

The TAP steering committees played a strategic role in the implementation of the program. Appointed by the building principal, the committee was representative of faculty interests and skills. It is helpful to have at least one skeptic on the committee who provides a different perspective and who knows what resistant teachers might be thinking.

District plans are to implement TAP in all six high schools and to complete a transition of leadership in each school from full-time or part-time TAP coordinators to a steering committee of teachers and counselors. More emphasis will be placed on advisory group sessions and the scheduling of daily TAP meetings.

What Advice Do You Have for Those Who Are Starting?

A steering committee is an important first step. The committee not only plans and designs, but it is the gauge for support and assessment and gives teachers ownership of TAP.

Staff development and lead planning time are essential elements of success. Teacher resistance can be addressed when effective training programs are available. Public relations with parents and community can make changes easier and should not be overlooked.

Between PEP in the middle schools and TAP in the high schools, Pasco County Schools are making a concentrated effort to reach out to students and give them more individual attention. This teacher advisement system is a movement toward facilitative learning environments which emphasize the value of teacher-student relationships.

A steering committee is an important first step. The committee...gives teachers ownership of TAP.

Chapter 8

Florida's Model and Pilot Schools

Elizabeth Lawson

Introduction

Florida legislators have taken a most impressive stand in favor of teacher advisement programs. Under the leadership of Senator Curtis Peterson, the "Teachers As Advisors Act" was passed in 1984. It first provided state funds for pilot and model teacher advisor programs (TAP) at the high school level. Three years later, additional appropriations were made available for model school projects at the middle school level. Between 1984 and 1989 approximately 25 million dollars have been appropriated for development and implementation of TAP in Florida schools.

This significant piece of legislation has received national attention from educators. First, it recognized the value of teacher advisement programs in the secondary schools. It emphasized that teachers can play an important role in guidance and outlined some minimum expectations. It was a major commitment for statewide adoption of an innovative approach to school guidance.

Between 1984 and 1989 approximately 25 million dollars have been appropriated for development and implementation of TAP in Florida schools.

High School TAP: Pilot and Model School Project

The primary intent of the TAP model projects from the onset was to help high school students cope with higher academic requirements for graduation, which had been passed in response to reports that our nation was at risk because of low educational standards. It was surmised that by having a teacher work directly with a small number of students, more students would be given personal attention. Counselor-student ratios were running as high as 1:400 or more. Other specialists had even higher ratios. TAP was designed for teacher-student ratios of less than 1:30.

Too many students move through four years of high school unaware of the school's offerings and, sadly, without much awareness of themselves or their own personal strengths and individual worth. It is the underlying belief of the teacher advisor program that the worth of the individual is of utmost importance and that every student deserves the attention of a caring, informed adult. Students need to have access to an advisor who is capable of monitoring academic progress and helping them make day-to-day decisions. In addition, advisors can refer students, when necessary, to the proper helpful resources when they themselves do not have answers or are limited in what they can do. The advisor becomes advocate and mentor: The one adult who has access to information and knows more about his or her advisees than anyone else in the school (Lawson, 1989).

It is the underlying belief of the teacher advisor program that the worth of the individual is of utmost importance.

The Beginning

In June of 1984 the Teachers As Advisors Act was passed (Section 230.23.1, Florida Statutes). Approximately 2.5 million dollars were appropriated for high school pilot projects. Dr. Jack Jenkins, P. K. Yonge Laboratory School, University of Florida, worked as a consultant to the Florida DOE and helped conceptualize the pilot school project. Individual schools from the 67 counties were encouraged to voluntarily submit to the Florida State Department of Education, Student Services Division, proposed programs designed to implement TAP in the district schools.

In September of 1984, 54 high schools submitted proposals and 39 were awarded grants. Priority was given to schools in which all teachers participated as advisors. Schools were given some leeway in terms of organization, but all programs had some minimum provisions, including:

Priority was given to schools in which all teachers participated as advisors.

1. Meeting the needs of disadvantaged and minority students.
2. Not exceeding a ratio of 30 students per one teacher advisor.
3. Having advisors meet a minimum of 30 minutes per advisee every 6 weeks.

4. Having advisors contact parents or guardians of students, especially those struggling academically.

As the program expanded during the next four years, some conditions for being awarded a grant were dropped or modified. More room was made for meeting advisees in groups and there was less insistence that teacher advisors spend no less than half their work time as classroom teachers. This enabled some schools to use more school personnel (such as counselors, media specialists, assistant principals, and resource teachers) to reduce the number of students in an advisory group. Meeting students individually was considered of utmost importance and a primary difference between high school and middle school teacher advisement programs. In addition, preventive or developmental guidance for all students was recognized as a valid concept.

The legislature continued its support of pilot and model programs by increasing appropriations each year. In September of 1985, 75 schools submitted proposals, of which 44 were given grants for the next calendar year, including the original 39 schools. By January of 1987, 54 out of 90 schools were awarded grants totaling more than 2.623 million dollars.

In January of 1988, 57 of 100 schools submitting proposals received grants for a total of 5.3 million dollars (an average cost of $37.67 per student). These project schools were located in 33 of 67 counties in Florida and served a population of 82,630 students. Three schools were eliminated from the project for not meeting standards and eight new schools were added. Data used for evaluation were based on 54 of these 57 schools.

Based on a survey of outcomes and favorable reports, the Florida legislature continued its support. In January of 1989, 102 high schools were funded and in the spring of 1989, 6.2 million dollars were appropriated for even further expansion.

Participating Schools

The project schools ranged in size from 145 students in a rural Franklin County school to 2,803 in metropolitan Dade County. Minority student enrollment across all schools was about 33 percent and a total of 26,000 minority students

Meeting students individually was considered of utmost importance and a primary difference between high school and middle school teacher advisement programs.

were part of the project. Of 54 project schools reporting, there was a fairly even distribution by size:

Size by Population	Number in Project
Below 500	8
501 - 1,000	10
1,001 - 1,500	12
1,501 - 2,000	10
Above 2,000	14

The average advisor-student ratio among the schools was about 1:18. The largest ratio in a school was 1:24 and the smallest was 1:8. One school failed to meet the minimum requirement of 30 minutes of contact per student each six weeks and was dropped from the project.

Fifty percent of the schools reported that advisors met with advisees on a daily basis and then for extended group meetings as needed. Setting aside more time to meet with students was a general trend in the pilot schools over the four-year period. Some schools reported group meetings of 30 to 50 minutes on a weekly, biweekly, monthly or six-week basis. However, for schools that were later added to the project the trend was proposals where advisory group meetings were held on a daily basis. This may have resulted from statewide training programs and the apparent success that schools with more extended time were having with students.

All but one school met the requirement of contacting parents of low performing students. A total of 143 professionals, other than teachers, served as advisors in the schools. For example, ten principals served as advisors. Assistant principals, media specialists, and counselors were also listed among nonclassroom teachers who had advisory groups.

Staff Development

The funds obtained from the grants were primarily used for staff development, which was an ongoing activity in all the project schools. Formal inservice programs were conducted in most of the schools during the school year with various topics selected by the steering committee, the coordinator, or principal. Almost 4,000 teachers participated in inservice training during the 1988 school year and another 1,000 attended summer inservice institutes.

Setting aside more time to meet with students was a general trend in the pilot schools over the four-year period.

The inservice programs were designed to introduce teachers to TAP, extend their knowledge and skills, and help them think about how to manage their advisory times. Preparatory inservice sessions were conducted by TAP coordinators and school counselors in 70 percent of the schools. One interesting trend was to involve more student services staff as trainers after programs were established and the teachers were oriented, thus depending less on outside consultants.

Topics for specific staff development activities varied, with knowledge of academic requirements at the top of the list. Teachers learned about state and local graduation requirements, district pupil progression plans, and overall school curriculum. In the second and third years, schools moved on to such areas as conferencing skills, group dynamics, drug and alcohol abuse, child abuse, AIDS, cultural awareness, and study skills. Learning styles also became a popular topic for staff development.

The need for staff development is most significant during the initial planning and implementation of TAP. Staff development then evolves into a maintenance and renewal function to ensure advisor effectiveness and to orient new faculty. Some suggested phases of training, needs, expected outcomes, logistics, topics and resources are presented in Appendix D. It serves as an overview of the scope of staff development for TAP in Florida.

One interesting trend was to involve more student services staff as trainers after programs were established....

Monitoring and Evaluating

During the first two years consultants from the Florida Department of Education talked with school personnel at the pilot schools and made on-site visits. Monitoring and assessment in the schools was considered to be ongoing and an essential component of advisement. While advisors were to evaluate their own objectives, it was suggested that the steering committee, or a person designated by the principal, take responsibility for organizing assessment procedures.

Some successful measures which were taken to evaluate a program's progress were:

- surveys which allowed parents, students, and advisors to give input;
- advisor logs of parent/student conferences and phone contacts;

- compilation of measurable outcomes: grades, attendance, discipline referrals;
- input from team leaders and the steering committee;
- administrative interventions with ineffective advisors.

The Florida Department of Education surveyed all pilot schools in the fall of each year and compiled a final report. The reports provided some feedback to practitioners and included general suggestions for modifications for the faculty and staff of participating schools. The reports also offered information to various committees of the State Legislature, the State Board of Education, and the State Commissioner of Education.

Teacher advisors in the original pilot schools gained experience over the four years and many of them became convinced that TAP was a valuable experience for students. This trend was aptly described in one state evaluation report:

> TAP provides an organized vehicle through which to accomplish what great, caring teachers have always been trying to accomplish. At our school, TAP has allowed all of our students to be "known." It has also allowed for all of our teachers to get to know our students on an individual basis. Advisors maintain close contact with the home which might not otherwise occur in most situations.

"At our school, TAP has allowed all of our students to be 'known.'"

The following excerpt was taken from another project report:

> The activities provided through the TAP Program promote a positive self-image and an assured self-concept. These activities also insure that every student is aware of district policies and requirements relating to attendance and grades. Students are tracked academically so that they always are aware of their current status. Referrals to school counselors and other agencies has increased since TAP was implemented, allowing students to resolve some of the problems leading to poor attendance and potential dropouts. One of the most important ways that TAP influences the dropout and attendance rate is by providing each student a significant adult on campus with whom to identify.

Assessing the Outcomes of TAP

In 1988 the DOE's Evaluation Report not only looked at reports from the previous year but relied on four survey instruments. The first two were directed to building principals and TAP coordinators. The third instrument was administered to a 2.5 percent sample of students (N = 1,958) in the pilot schools and the fourth to a 13 percent sample of teachers-advisors (N = 562). All of the instruments asked for information about implementation and outcomes.

When data were examined it appeared that TAP had a positive impact on students. Credit was given in evaluation reports for improved academic achievement, a reduction in failing grades, and an increase in higher test scores.

More specifically, information cited improved test scores on state assessment instruments, the Preliminary Scholastic Aptitude Test (PSAT), the Scholastic Aptitude Test (SAT), and the American College Test (ACT). Spruce Creek High School in Volusia County showed steady increases in the ACT composite scores over the three years from the time when TAP was implemented and a 40 percent increase in the number of students who took the test. Of 14 schools completing their second and third years in the project, seven indicated improvement in academic achievement since the inception of TAP, as measured by increased grade point averages, improved standardized test scores, and a reduction in the number of failures.

For example, Pahokee High School in Palm Beach County showed an increase of six percent in the number of students attaining a 2.0 grade point average or better. The failure rate at Ernest Ward High School in Escambia County decreased from 3.17 percent of the student body in 1984 to .54 percent in 1988. The ACT scores at Miami Beach High School in Dade County, increased 28 points on the mathematics section and 31 points on the verbal section in three years. Rickards High School in Leon County showed a decrease in grade failures from 50 to 44 percent of students failing one or more courses.

More students took college entrance examinations and this was attributed to encouragement, support, and more information reaching students during advisory group meetings. There was more monitoring of student progress by advisors and this was corroborated by 61 percent of the students surveyed. Of the teachers surveyed, 73 percent

Credit was given [to TAP] in evaluation reports for improved academic achievement, a reduction in failing grades, and an increase in higher test scores.

More students took college entrance examinations....

indicated that they kept report cards on their advisees as a regular part of their responsibilities. When asked, more than half of all the teachers reported that their influence caused improved grades in at least one of their advisees and 46 percent believed they influenced several of their advisees to improve their grades.

Student attendance in all participating schools improved 44 percent. Fifty percent of the schools completing their fourth year reported improved attendance. Surprisingly, only 30 percent of the teachers thought they had positively influenced their advisees attendance.

In terms of student attitudes, the fourth year project schools reported an 87 percent improvement and the rest listed an improvement of 75.4 percent, based on an attitude survey. Of the teacher advisors, 57 percent said they had positively influenced their advisees' attitudes toward school and this outcome was related to improved student-teacher relationships.

Of the third and fourth year schools in the project, 59 percent described how increased involvement of the advisors with advisees through daily meetings and regularly scheduled conferences led to a reduction in the number of school dropouts. There was an improvement of 13 percent from 1987 to 1988. Sixty-one percent of the students said that the advisement program enabled them to learn about graduation requirements and career opportunities, both of which tended to give them a purpose for remaining in school. Appointments to see school counselors were expedited, credit checks gave more students immediate and timely information, and teacher progress reports received more immediate attention.

Students like TAP and 74 percent of the surveyed students wanted TAP to continue at their school. While not all students supported the program, there were numerous student statements from all schools which indicated that TAP had made a positive difference with them and their peers.

Middle School TAP: Pilot and Model Schools Project

Based on the preliminary reports of the success of TAP in the project high schools, the Florida legislature funded a similar model school grant project for middle schools. In June of 1987 approximately 472,000 dollars was awarded to four model schools and 18 pilot schools. This appropriation was doubled in 1988 to include five model and 36 pilot schools. The 1989 funds reached 2.8 million dollars for a projected ten model and 100 or more pilot schools.

This project was designed keeping in mind that exemplary advisor-advisee programs already existed in many of Florida's middle schools. Florida had been a national leader in restructuring junior high schools to middle schools during the 1960s and 1970s, and TAP was considered an integrated part of middle school philosophy and structure. The rationale for TAP and its implementation in a high school was, in general, the same for a middle school. Advisor roles and responsibilities were essentially the same, although guidance activities in advisory groups were related to different stages of development.

Therefore, proposals for model schools were sought by the Florida DOE and funds were awarded to model middle school sites to be used to train pilot school personnel. The model schools agreed to release time for the principal and selected staff members to allow for on-site visitations from the pilot schools and for travel to those schools for staff development.

The pilot schools spent approximately six months planning for inservice and implementation of TAP. This included:

- Site visits by pilot school staff to model schools.
- Subsequent presentations from model school staff to pilot school faculty (awareness and motivation).
- Selection of a school-based steering committee, including a "negative" teacher or two.
- The selection of one or two model schools with which to work closely.
- Two or three days of immersion activities at the model school site, with model school faculty members guiding visiting committees through all aspects of advisement.
- Sharing information gained with the pilot school faculty.
- Subsequent visits by model school principal and coordinator for more follow-up and inservice.

...funds were awarded to model middle school sites to be used to train pilot school personnel.

- Extensive input from pilot faculty to their steering committee as they plan for summer inservice prior to implementing the program in the fall of the school year.

TAP: A Grass-roots Endeavor

Although it was logical that TAP for students should begin at an early age, the case for advisement in the high schools was compelling. Fewer teacher advisor programs existed in the high schools and the need to provide more guidance services at that level was so evident that it captured the attention of legislators. Thus, legislation and appropriations were first directed to high schools.

Some discussion ensued in the legislature about legally mandating TAP for all secondary schools. However, such a mandate was viewed as undermining the integrity of the philosophy and rationale of the program; and, it would likely create more teacher resistance. Teacher support was essential to the success of the program.

TAP requires that it be a grass-roots endeavor. It needs to be investigated, developed, implemented, assessed and revised by school staff and faculty, based on the needs and interests of the students served. Moreover, it appears that the successful outcomes of TAP sell the concept to others. As one high school principal reported in a Florida DOE Final Report (Jenkins, 1989):

> Attendance is improved, the overall G.P.A. has increased five percent. The failure rate is down, parents are coming to school to become involved, and students are beginning to individualize their advisement time, based on their needs for that week. Advisement has become a serious, useful and fun time for students and advisors. When positive programs are in place, such as TAP, and students feel that they are cared about and worthwhile, then good things are bound to happen! (p. 219)

...the case for advisement in the high schools was compelling.

...the successful outcomes of TAP sell the concept to others.

Advisement has become a serious, useful and fun time for students and advisors.

Chapter 9

Teacher Questions and Staff Development

Signs of Resistance or Legitimate Concerns?

Clearly, one of the most difficult parts of implementing TAP in schools across the nation rests in the knowledge, attitude, and commitment of teachers. This may be surprising to those who realize that the philosophy, goals, and procedures of TAP are central to the mission of any school and that the program is related directly to helping students learn more effectively and efficiently. But, many teachers have questions which must be answered.

Some common questions which have been asked at staff development workshops are:

- What makes us qualified to do this?
- What about kids with behavior problems?
- What about sensitive issues where I'm not an expert?
- How can TAP work for kids who don't even want to be in school?
- I'm not a counselor, so how do I do group guidance?
- Doesn't this program take time away from teaching?
- What am I expected to do?
- Is this faculty honestly going to try to make it work?
- I already do this, so why do we need a special period for it?
- It's an extra preparation and aren't we already working hard enough?
- What do you do with kids who don't want our help?
- What if we don't like a guidance activity?
- Do we have to follow the guidance curriculum?

...many teachers have questions which must be answered.

- Do you really think we can make a difference with some of these kids?
- What are our legal responsibilities?
- Who's idea was this?
- What about those kids who are stuck with advisors who really don't support the program?

Some resistance and lack of support result from teachers misunderstanding their responsibilities in the program. Most already believe that they are overloaded with teaching assignments and duties. Many are strong advocates of focusing primarily on academics. They argue that if they had more time to work with students in their courses, then failure rates would be reduced and achievement would be higher. This case becomes debatable when we take note of the large number of students who lack school success skills and the increasing number who are losing interest in school and dropping out.

There are some teachers who are threatened by close relationships with students.

There are some teachers who are threatened by close relationships with students. These teachers might know their subjects and have well-organized lesson plans but prefer to lecture and demonstrate to students. Relying less on class discussions, these teachers fear they will lose control when students are encouraged to talk about their own ideas, interests, and concerns. Many of these same teachers feel uncomfortable working with students who need special attention. They believe they lack the skills to work with personal or social problems and that these matters should be the responsibility of someone else.

A large number of dedicated teachers simply want to know more about the program before they are willing to commit their energy and time. The idea may be appealing, but they view it as a trade-off. Something must give way to making time for TAP. These teachers offer a healthy skepticism and many become avid supporters of TAP after they have participated in effective staff development training and had first-hand experiences with the program.

When teachers dislike the concept and simply go along with it, TAP is likely to fail.

When teachers dislike the concept and simply go along with it, TAP is likely to fail. It also fails when teachers see it as an imposition on them and see no gains in terms of student achievement, positive attitudes, or a better working environment. When teachers have no choice but to participate, success may be limited until they are won over through the positive outcomes. Or, they simply go through the motions and deny young people needed and valuable experiences.

Negative teachers, who are unwilling to change their attitude or to learn new skills, may be a perfect match for students who are disruptive or are discipline problems during teacher advisory periods. These two groups—teachers and students—might be put into one large group, perhaps a study hall. Then, counselors work with target students from this pool, helping them make adjustments which put them back in an advisory group. Ironically, a few of these same teachers can reach some troublesome students with whom others have not been successful if they will only try.

Teacher questions should not be dismissed as irrelevant. They are all valid concerns and deserve a response. Each question is asked to set matters straight. Even though some are not really questions but statements, and even though some probably have hidden—or not so hidden—agendas behind them, they must be answered to the satisfaction of the entire faculty and staff. After all, TAP is their program and they are the key players.

Teacher questions should not be dismissed as irrelevant. They are all valid concerns and deserve a response.

Common Questions

Although many questions may have been addressed already in the preceding chapters, let's take a closer look at a few of them.

What do I do since I can't give a grade? Some teachers fear that students will be uncooperative since they are not graded for the experience, even for citizenship. These teachers believe that students will view TAP as less important than classes where they receive credit for their participation and effort. Although grades are not assigned, advisors can still use their own recording system to compliment or confront students when appropriate. Feedback from group members is important both in terms of special recognition and when confronting attitudes and behaviors.

How do I maintain control? The informal atmosphere of TAP, at times, causes some teachers to think they are getting dangerously close to being out of control. Advisory groups have positively stated rules and procedures. Advisors must be flexible but they can also seize upon "rule breaking" as a moment for timely discussions and teaching.

Advisory groups have positively stated rules and procedures.

> *TAP is an opportunity for timely learning and every session does not have to weigh heavy with adolescent problems and issues.*

Getting students to be sensitive and respect the rights of others is a desired outcome of developmental guidance.

What do you do if the kids won't talk? It takes some time to establish a close working relationship with each advisee and with the advisory group. Group dynamics are influenced by group members and the advisor's leadership style. TAP is an opportunity for timely learning and every session does not have to weigh heavy with adolescent problems and issues. It is also a time for making new friends, developing a support group, and having fun. As group members experience respect, interest, and caring from one another, there is a greater willingness to share ideas and to be open to experience.

What if an activity doesn't work? Not all structured learning activities are guaranteed to be successful. Some may even be questionable, such as those which force students to make only negative choices. An activity is only a means to an end. It is not the final goal. Rather, advisors must learn how to facilitate discussions which result from participating in an activity, whether it turns out as planned or not. There are always points to be discussed, opinions, related behaviors, and factors which influence group interaction. If something is not going well, then stop. Talk about what students are experiencing and what changes might make the activity or discussion better.

What if an advisee shares something too personal? A professional judgment is made as to whether the advisee should continue to explore the matter with the peer group or if the advisor should interrupt and recommend that the advisee delay talking about it any further at that moment, until a private conference can be held. Or, the advisor may say, "Before we go on, is this something you want to continue to share with us? By continuing, you're saying that you trust us and believe that we will be understanding." This may slow the advisee down for a moment in order to assess the situation. If the advisee wishes to continue, then the advisor's own comfort level and skills are going to determine what happens next. Advisors may refer students to school counselors. But, it should be remembered the advisory group was perceived by the student as a place to be heard, to think about the problem, and to consider alternatives.

> *...the advisory group was perceived by the student as a place to be heard, to think about the problem, and to consider alternatives.*

When will I find time to plan? If the advisory group meets each day, only two days are typically used for group guidance lessons or activities. The advisor might use the other three days, perhaps during silent reading, to review or study a guidance unit and activity. Otherwise, preparation time will come from a teacher's regular preparation period. This issue is more of a concern to junior and high school faculties. Middle school educators, by educational philosophy and team organizational structure, view advisory groups as part of their regular assignment. Without some form of TAP, a middle school schedule is incomplete.

Staff Development and Training Workshops

The questions raised by supportive and nonsupportive teachers and staff must be respected and given a response in staff development and training workshops. Some may be responded to in a question-answer format. But, this is rarely enough. Almost all of the meaningful and satisfactory answers come through learning activities in a workshop and actual experience with advisees in an advisory group.

No amount of study and reassurance by a principal or steering committee will resolve all the issues behind the questions. Unlimited planning time and careful attention to details will not eliminate all start-up problems. There are no guarantees. Some teachers will be successful immediately while others will struggle for awhile and wonder if they can be effective advisors.

Staff development is viewed by almost every school which has TAP as the most critical factor for success. First, it brings the faculty together so that basic questions can be answered and organizational logistics can be clarified. Second, the roles of advisors and other personnel are examined, and teachers have a better idea of what is expected of them. Third, specific advisor skills, such as conferencing and leading group discussions, receive attention. Group activities are studied and facilitative skills are learned, relearned, and renewed. Demonstrations help and practicing the skills together is even more helpful. Additional questions are asked and answers come from both trainers and the participants. Finally, the faculty and staff experience an

Staff development is viewed by almost every school which has TAP as the most critical factor for success.

added cohesiveness and closeness as a result of training workshops. Beyond being inspired and becoming more knowledgeable, participants gain a feeling of self-confidence and develop a willingness to try.

Perhaps the basic question that every participant in a staff development workshop wants answered is: "What's in it for me?" Workshops about TAP are no different. Teachers want to know: "Is this going to make my job easier?" "Will I get more done in a shorter period of time, or is this just another hassle?" "What satisfaction will I get? What support will I have?"

A second question to be answered at a conscious or unconscious level is almost always: "Do I have to do this?" The answer "Yes" may result from being inspired and sensing that the program is truly the heart of guidance and a way to help students learn more. When the answer "Yes" comes as a directive from an enthusiastic administration, there still may be initial sighs and expressions about being overburdened. Without a choice, many advisors simply go about the task of doing the best job they can. Some outstanding and influential advisors, who made positive differences with students who needed their help, may have wanted to say "No" in the beginning.

Finally, "Okay, if I have to do this, how do you go about it?" The focus of most staff development workshops is increased knowledge, skills, awareness, and some general directions.

Some outstanding and influential advisors...may have wanted to say "No" in the beginning.

Communication and Interpersonal Skills

Improved communication and interpersonal skills are primary objectives in training workshops. Advisors are asked to be facilitators, to slow down and listen carefully to students, and to encourage them to share ideas. Probably every teacher employed has been through some kind of workshop or conference where the importance of interpersonal relationships and communication skills was emphasized. "If you have been to one, you have probably been to two or three," said one teacher.

These terms are tossed around so flippantly at times and treated so pedantically, teachers may groan when they hear that a consultant is going to work with them on "how to listen and talk with students." A high school teacher remarked, "We do this all day. It's our job. So, what else is new?"

What's new to many teachers are simple communication models which help them best use their advisory time. These have been presented elsewhere and there are many models which may be useful. For the most part, however, teacher advisors need specific skills related to specific helping strategies. Advisors want to know what to say in given situations. They like to explore hypothetical cases: "What do you do if...?" "What happens when...?" "What if the student...?"

...teacher advisors need specific skills related to specific helping strategies.

For example, the communication model developed by Wittmer and Myrick (1989) focuses on six basic facilitative responses which can be used with advisees individually or in groups. Advisors are cautioned about the use of low facilitative responses and their probable effects. By increasing the frequency of the high facilitative responses in TAP, the advisor is more likely to have a positive influence. The high facilitative responses are: feeling-focused responses (pleasant or unpleasant feelings); clarifying or summarizing (events or ideas); open questions (especially how or what), complimenting and confronting (feedback); linking (pairing ideas or feelings); and, simple acknowledgments (thanking someone for a contribution). The low facilitative responses, which are less likely to be used except when timely, include: advice or evaluation; analysis or interpretation; reassuring or supportive statements which quickly dismiss a person's feelings; and closed (yes/no) questions.

Next, advisors want to know how to use these skills when advisees talk with them about problems or special interests. High facilitative responses can keep the focus on the advisee's personal decision making and problem solving abilities. In addition to communication skills, teachers learn through staff development how they can guide their advisees through the maze of school forms and the tasks of career and educational planning. Advisors learn to explain graduation requirements and to direct advisees to resources.

One successful staff development program was pioneered in Sarasota County, Florida (Myrick, Highland & Highland,1986). In this plan, an external consultant met for three days with 50 teachers and counselors, ten from each of the five middle schools in the district. During the first half of the workshop, the participants listened to concepts related to a facilitative communication model, saw related skills demonstrated, and then practiced them. In the second half of the workshop, the participants were divided into five teams of co-leaders for their respective schools and learned how to lead training modules related to the same training they had just experienced. They followed a trainer's handbook which outlined ten 30-minute modules.

The participants then returned to their schools and helped arrange on-site staff development experiences for the other teachers and counselors in their buildings. Working in five teams of co-leaders, with each team responsible for one or two modules, they were able to provide timely inservice to their faculties. Because teachers themselves rather than an outside consultant were the leaders, the staff development experience took on greater credibility. Co-leaders took the position that they were not experts but wanted to explore the ideas and skills with their training groups (about 6–8 teachers in each group). Hypothetical cases were discussed and teachers were encouraged to try the ideas in their regular classes. Follow-up discussions led to more clarification and practice.

The outcomes of this training program led other school districts to organize similar staff development programs for their teachers. For instance, Huntsville, Alabama, modified the Sarasota plan and took nine school faculties through eight modules in the spring of a school year. Green Bay, Wisconsin modified both plans and arrived at a similar but unique plan in which teams of co-leaders from a school presented eight modules to a faculty. Orange County Schools, in Orlando, Florida also piloted a staff development program which emphasized training teams and trainer notebooks for their IMPACT program in 18 middle schools.

The Florida Department of Education has been actively involved in supporting staff development and inservice training workshops for TAP in the state's middle and high schools. The more than 100 pilot and model schools awarded grants for teacher advisor programs will spend a large proportion of their funds on staff development. The Florida DOE staff development outline emphasizes phases, logistics, and resources for a school district. It contains recommendations for beginning and veteran programs.

The more than 100 pilot and model schools awarded grants for teacher advisor programs will spend a large proportion of their funds on staff development.

Drawing attention to expected outcomes, it also suggests inservice sessions and topics. It is hard to improve upon the recommended flow of events (see Appendix D).

The final question, then, is: "When should we start?" The answer is "Now!" Decide on some next steps which will move the school system or school toward a teacher advisement program. A great many questions cannot even be asked until some first steps are taken to get the program started. Many of the answers will come from teachers themselves, as they creatively use this new approach to meeting the developmental guidance needs of their students.

The final question, then, is: "When should we start?" The answer is "Now!"

References

Alexander, W. M., & George, P. S. (1981). *The exemplary middle school.* New York: Holt, Rinehart and Winston.

Alexander, W. M., & McEwin, C. K. (1989). *Earmarks of schools in the middle: A research report.* Boone, NC: Appalachian State University.

Alexander, W. M., Williams, E., Compton, M., Hines, V., Prescott, D., & Kealy, R. (1969). *The emergent middle school.* New York: Holt, Rinehart and Winston.

Bergmann, S., & Baxter, J. (1983). Building a guidance program and advisory concept for early adolescents. *NASSP Bulletin, 67*(463), 49–55.

Bohlinger, T. (1976). Middle school guidance: Problems in comprehensiveness and implementation. *Middle School Counselor, 7*(4), 7–22.

Carnegie Council on Adolescent Development. (1989, Summer). *Turning points: Preparing American youth for the 21st century* (Special Task Force Report). Washington, DC: Carnegie Corporation.

Daresh, J. C., & Pautsch, T. R. (1983). A successful teacher-advisor program. *Middle School Journal, 14*(3), 3–13.

Flanders, N. (1965). *Teacher influence, pupil attitudes, and achievement.* Washington, DC: U.S. Department of Health, Education, and Welfare.

Gardner, D. (1983). *A nation at risk: The imperative for educational reform.* Washington, DC: U.S. Department of Education.

George, P. S. (1986). The counselor and modern middle-level schools: New roles in new schools. *School Counselor, 33*(3), 178–188.

Goldberg, M. F. (1977). House group: A guidance role for the teacher. *NASSP Bulletin, 61*(410), 61–64.

Harris, L. (1985). *Metropolitan Life poll of the American teacher.* New York: Metropolitan Life Foundation.

Henderson, P., & La Forge, J. (1989). The role of the middle school counselor in teacher-advisor programs. *School Counselor, 36*(5), 348-351.

James, M. (1986). *Advisor-advisee programs: Why, what and how.* Columbus, OH: National Middle School Association.

Jenkins, J. (1977). The teacher-advisor: An old solution looking for a problem. *NASSP Bulletin, 61*(410), 29–34.

Jenkins, J. (1989). *Teachers as advisors: Program evaluation report.* Tallahassee: Florida Department of Education.

Johnson, R. L., & Salmon, S. J. (1979). Caring and counseling: Shared tasks in advisement schools. *Personnel and Guidance Journal, 57,* 474–477.

Kornik, J. (1984). Counselor-specialist and teacher-counselor: A plan for the future. *School Counselor, 31,* 241–248.

Klausmeier, H. J., Lipham, J. M., & Daresh, J. C. (1983). *The renewal and improvement of secondary education.* London, England: University Press of America.

Lawson, E. (Ed.). (1989). *Florida's teachers as advisors program.* Tallahassee: Florida Department of Education.

Lipsitz, J. (1984). *Successful schools for young adolescents.* New Brunswick, NJ: Transaction, Inc.

Mills, H. (1985). A participative program for developing an advisor-advisee program. *Middle School Journal, VXVII*(4), 6–7.

Myrick, R. D. (1987). *Developmental guidance and counseling: A practical approach.* Minneapolis: Educational Media Corporation.

Myrick, R. D., & Erney, T. (1978). *Youth helping youth.* Minneapolis: Educational Media Corporation.

Myrick, R. D., Highland, M., & Highland, W. (1986). Preparing teachers to be advisors. *Middle School Journal, 17,* 15–16.

Myrick, R. D. (1989). *Developmental guidance and counseling: A practical approach.* Minneapolis: Educational Media Corporation.

National Governors' Association. (1989). *America in transition: The international frontier* (Report of the Task Force on Children). Washington, DC: Author.

Patterson, L. E., & Sikler, J. R. (1974). Teachers as helpers: Extending guidance contact. *School Counselor, 22,* 113–120.

Pilkington, R. A., & Jarmin, H. R. (1977). Teacher-advisor or teacher-counselor—Is there a difference? *NASSP Bulletin, 61*(410), 80–83.

Purkey, W. (1970). *Self-concept and school achievement.* Englewood Cliffs, NJ: Prentice-Hall.

Sarasota County Schools. (1982). *PRIME TIME handbook.* Sarasota, FL: Author.

Shockley, R., Schumacher, R., & Smith, D. (1984). Teacher advisory programs—Strategies for successful implementation. *NASSP Bulletin, 68*(473), 69–74.

Tamminen, A. (1976). Teacher-advisors: Where there's skill there's a way. *Personnel and Guidance Journal, 55,* 39–42.

Thornburg, H. D. (1986). The counselor's impact on middle-grade students. *School Counselor, 33*(3), 170–177.

Trump, J. L. (1977). Are counselors meeting student and teacher needs? *NASSP Bulletin, 61*(410), 26–28.

Wittmer, J., & Myrick, R. D. (1980). *Facilitative teaching.* Minneapolis: Educational Media Corporation.

Wittmer, J., & Myrick, R. D. (1989). *Teacher as facilitator.* Minneapolis: Educational Media Corporation.

Appendix A

Developmental Guidance Units—TAP

Unit 1: Getting Acquainted

To help advisor group members to know each other.
To build facilitative relationships within the group.
To lay the foundation for advisor-advisee group meetings.
To help advisees learn how to participate in a group.
To help advisees make positive transitions in school.
To review school handbook and school procedures.

Unit 2: Study Skills and Habits

To evaluate one's study skills and habits.
To develop effective time-management plans.
To learn and practice classroom listening skills.
To identify various tests and test-taking situations.
To learn ways to cope with test-anxiety.
To understand grade point average (GPA) and report cards.
To discuss school success skills.

Unit 3: Self-Assessment

To identify classroom behaviors related to achievement.
To identify one's strengths in classroom behaviors.
To identify classroom behaviors that need to be improved.
To assess teacher-student relationships.
To assess attitudes about school, self, and others.
To set goals and learn to monitor progress.
To develop an appreciation of individual differences.
To identify one's interests, abilities, and uniqueness.

Unit 4: Communication Skills

To identify and practice interpersonal skills related to the facilitative conditions and facilitative model.
To learn how to be sensitive and "tune in" to others.
To learn how to be a careful listener.
To learn how to clarify and explore ideas.
To learn how to ask and to respond to thoughtful questions.
To learn ways to compliment and to confront others.
To identify behaviors which block effective communication.
To learn how to be an effective group participant.
To learn how one's behavior has an effect on others.

Unit 5: Decision-Making and Problem-Solving

To learn models for decision-making and problem-solving.
To learn how to identify alternatives and consequences.
To identify common teen-age dilemmas and factors which influence decision-making and problem-solving.
To show how decision-making and problem-solving skills can be used at home and school.
To examine the consequences of not meeting school and family obligations and responsibilities.

Unit 6: Peer Relationships

To examine sex roles and sex stereotypes in society.
To develop positive ways of interacting with peers.
To recognize the power of peer influence.
To assess one's self and peer relationships.
To learn how to develop friendships.
To learn ways to resist undesirable peer pressure.
To increase awareness of how personal needs and interests affect relationships.

Unit 7: Motivation

To become more aware of one's interests, needs, and desires.

To recognize how one's self-esteem and attitudes are related to the way in which a goal is approached.
To recognize the value of setting personal goals.
To differentiate between intrinsic and extrinsic rewards.
To identify motivational techniques, such as goal setting, monitoring, self-talk, action steps, and positive thinking.
To show how skills and practice are related to success.

Unit 8: Conflict/Resolution

To identify the nature of conflict, how and when it can occur.
To learn constructive ways of dealing with conflict.
To identify conflicts related to developmental stages of life.
To practice applying communication skills to conflict moments.
To identify how conflict/resolution skills can be applied with teachers, parents, or peers.

Unit 9: Wellness

To identify common health problems in our society.
To identify positive aspects of living a healthy life.
To discuss how exercise, nutrition, positive attitudes, and personal living habits can affect one's life.
To be aware of the characteristics of "high risk" people, such as: alcohol and drug abuse, suicide, and potential dropouts.
To examine the value of wellness and prevention strategies.
To examine the long-range consequences of abusive behaviors.
To develop and practice effective ways of coping with stress.

Unit 10: Career Development

To examine the effect of changing times on the world of work.
To recognize job opportunities and their value to society.

To identify how jobs, occupations, and careers are related to one's interests, needs, skills, and opportunities.
To identify tentative job goals.
To become aware of the factors that influence job choice.
To recognize how job goals are related to success in school.
To identify how job tasks relate to skills learned in school.

Unit 11: Educational Planning

To recognize options that are available for planning.
To illustrate the need to plan ahead.
To learn a language of educational planning (common terms).
To learn the sequence of academic courses.
To identify academic requirements and electives.
To develop an educational plan for middle or high school.
To register for next year's courses.

Unit 12: Community Involvement

To develop pride in the community.
To identify responsibilities of citizens in the community.
To see the value of volunteering for community service.
To identify ways in which young people can help make the community and neighborhoods better places to live.

Reprinted from Myrick, R. D. (1989). *Developmental guidance and counseling: A practical approach.* Minneapolis, MN: Educational Media Corporation.

Appendix B

Roles of School Personnel in TAP

The Advisor's Role

1. To know each advisee on a personal basis, establishing a friendly and caring working relationship.
2. To follow up with advisees regarding academic progress, grade reports, discipline referrals, special concerns, and general school information.
3. To know and confer with parents/guardians of advisees, facilitating communication between home and school.
4. To build group cohesiveness among a group of advisees so that they might be resources to one another.
5. To use group activities to help obtain developmental guidance goals and objectives.
6. To help identify student guidance needs and make recommendations to the school's guidance committee.
7. To consult with other school personnel (e.g., counselors and social workers) about guidance needs of advisees.
8. To seek assistance for advisees whose needs are beyond the limits of TAP or skills of the advisor.

The School Counselor's Role

1. To facilitate and help coordinate the initiation, implementation and development of TAP.
2. To consult with advisors regarding guidance activities and special needs of students.
3. To serve as a resource to advisors, modeling skills and co-leading guidance activities in advisory groups when appropriate.
4. To encourage and facilitate staff development for advisors.

5. To receive and follow-up with student referrals through individual and small group counseling.
6. To help coordinate, if not train, peer facilitators to assist advisors and advisees in TAP.
7. To present special guidance units to students in advisory group meetings when appropriate.
8. To serve as a liaison between advisors and district personnel who can assist students with special needs.
9. To be a member, if assigned, of the TAP steering committee.

The Principal's Role

1. To provide leadership for TAP.
2. To organize and coordinate the overall development of TAP.
3. To monitor, review, assess, and evaluate all aspects of TAP related to TAP goals and objectives.
4. To arrange for the necessary time, materials, and facilities to implement TAP.
5. To visit and speak with advisory groups, showing support and meeting with students as time is available.
6. To consult with advisors regarding advisee needs when appropriate, giving assistance when referrals are necessary.
7. To arrange for staff development for advisors.

Appendix C

Sample Advisement Telephone Call

"Hello, this is _____. I am your (son's, daughter's) advisor for Prime Time. I wanted to call and tell you how pleased I am to have _____ in my advisement group this year. I will be especially interested in keeping up with _____'s progress in school this year.

Do you have any question at this time that I could help you with? (response from parent). It is nice to talk with you. Please feel free to call me if you have any information that will affect _____'s schoolwork or behavior.

Thank you for taking the time to talk with me today. I look forward to meeting you at the Back to School Night on _____. Goodbye."

Reprinted from *PRIME TIME Handbook*, Sarasota County Schools, Sarasota, Florida.

Appendix D: TAP Staff Development

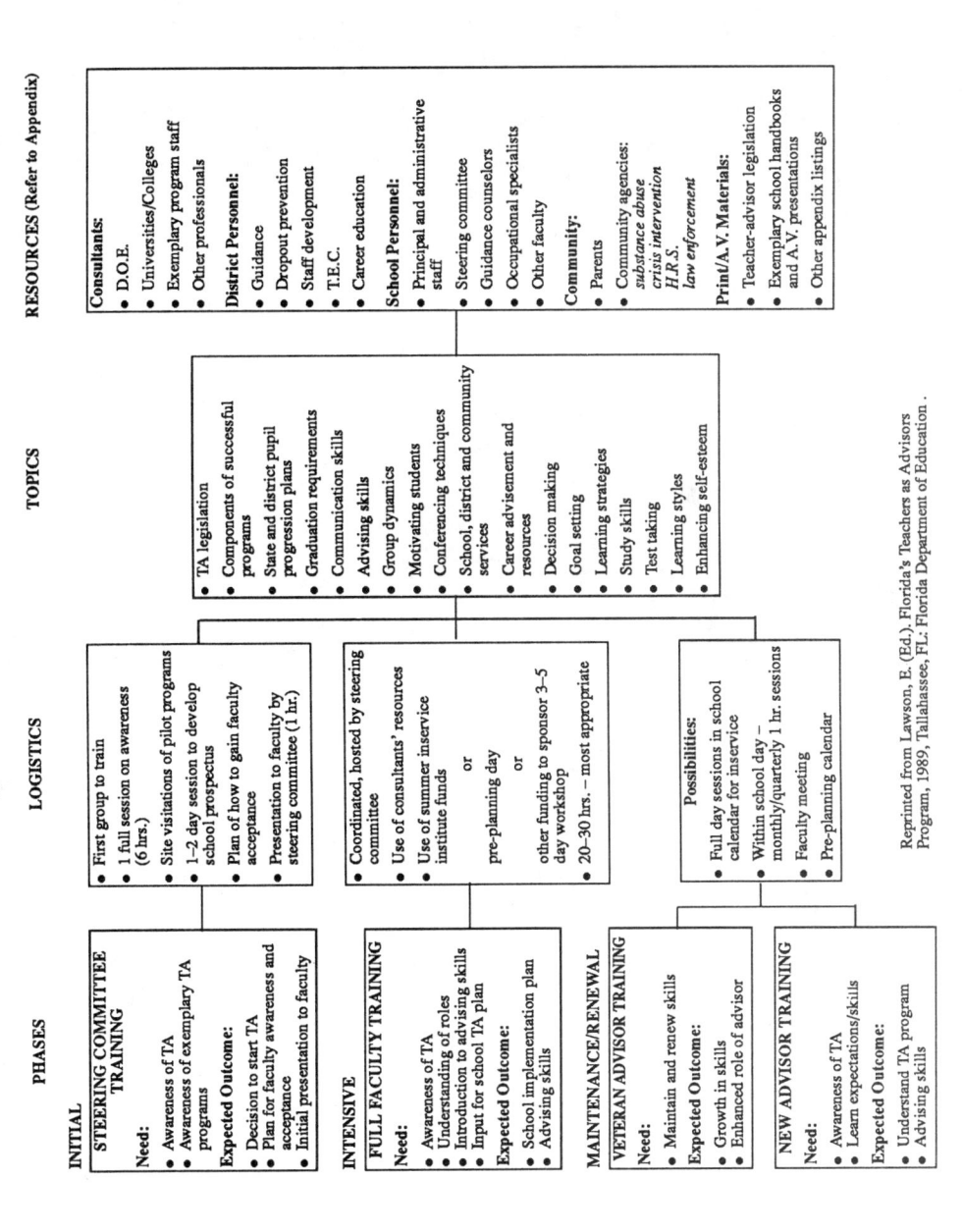

PHASES	LOGISTICS	TOPICS	RESOURCES (Refer to Appendix)

INITIAL

STEERING COMMITTEE TRAINING

Need:
- Awareness of TA
- Awareness of exemplary TA programs

Expected Outcome:
- Decision to start TA
- Plan for faculty awareness and acceptance
- Initial presentation to faculty

Logistics:
- First group to train
- 1 full session on awareness (6 hrs.)
- Site visitations of pilot programs
- 1–2 day session to develop school prospectus
- Plan of how to gain faculty acceptance
- Presentation to faculty by steering committee (1 hr.)

INTENSIVE

FULL FACULTY TRAINING

Need:
- Awareness of TA
- Understanding of roles
- Introduction to advising skills
- Input for school TA plan

Expected Outcome:
- School implementation plan
- Advising skills

Logistics:
- Coordinated, hosted by steering committee
- Use of consultants' resources
- Use of summer inservice institute funds
  or
- pre-planning day
  or
- other funding to sponsor 3–5 day workshop
- 20–30 hrs. – most appropriate

MAINTENANCE/RENEWAL

VETERAN ADVISOR TRAINING

Need:
- Maintain and renew skills

Expected Outcome:
- Growth in skills
- Enhanced role of advisor

NEW ADVISOR TRAINING

Need:
- Awareness of TA
- Learn expectations/skills

Expected Outcome:
- Understand TA program
- Advising skills

Logistics Possibilities:
- Full day sessions in school calendar for inservice
- Within school day – monthly/quarterly 1 hr. sessions
- Faculty meeting
- Pre-planning calendar

TOPICS:
- TA legislation
- Components of successful programs
- State and district pupil progression plans
- Graduation requirements
- Communication skills
- Advising skills
- Group dynamics
- Motivating students
- Conferencing techniques
- School, district and community services
- Career advisement and resources
- Decision making
- Goal setting
- Learning strategies
- Study skills
- Test taking
- Learning styles
- Enhancing self-esteem

RESOURCES:

Consultants:
- D.O.E.
- Universities/Colleges
- Exemplary program staff
- Other professionals

District Personnel:
- Guidance
- Dropout prevention
- Staff development
- T.E.C.
- Career education

School Personnel:
- Principal and administrative staff
- Steering committee
- Guidance counselors
- Occupational specialists
- Other faculty

Community:
- Parents
- Community agencies: substance abuse crisis intervention H.R.S. law enforcement

Print/A.V. Materials:
- Teacher-advisor legislation
- Exemplary school handbooks and A.V. presentations
- Other appendix listings

Reprinted from Lawson, E. (Ed.). Florida's Teachers as Advisors Program, 1989, Tallahassee, FL: Florida Department of Education.